Detracking
for Excellence
and Equity

ASCD MEMBER BOOK

Many ASCD members received this book as a
member benefit upon its initial release.

Learn more at: **www.ascd.org/memberbooks**

Mixed Sources
Product group from well-managed
forests and recycled wood or fiber
www.fsc.org Cert no. BV-COC-070702
© 1996 Forest Stewardship Council

FSC

ASCD cares about Planet Earth.
This book has been printed on environmentally friendly paper.

Detracking
for Excellence
and Equity

Carol Corbett Burris

Delia T. Garrity

ASCD

Association for Supervision and Curriculum Development
Alexandria, Virginia USA

Association for Supervision and Curriculum Development
1703 N. Beauregard St. • Alexandria, VA 22311–1714 USA
Phone: 800-933-2723 or 703-578-9600 • Fax: 703-575-5400
Web site: www.ascd.org • E-mail: member@ascd.org
Author guidelines: www.ascd.org/write

Gene R. Carter, *Executive Director;* Nancy Modrak, *Publisher;* Julie Houtz, *Director of Book Editing & Production;* Katie Martin, *Project Manager;* Georgia Park, *Senior Graphic Designer;* Mike Kalyan, *Production Manager;* Cynthia Stock, *Typesetter;* Carmen Yuhas, *Production Specialist*

Printed in the United States of America. Cover art copyright © 2008 by ASCD. ASCD publications present a variety of viewpoints. The views expressed or implied in this book should not be interpreted as official positions of the Association.

All Web links in this book are correct as of the publication date below but may have become inactive or otherwise modified since that time. If you notice a deactivated or changed link, please e-mail books@ascd.org with the words "Link Update" in the subject line. In your message, please specify the Web link, the book title, and the page number on which the link appears.

ASCD Member Book, No. FY08-9 (August 2008, P). ASCD Member Books mail to Premium (P) and Select (S) members on this schedule: Jan., PS; Feb., P; Apr., PS; May, P; July, PS; Aug., P; Sept., PS; Nov., PS; Dec., P. Select membership was formerly known as Comprehensive membership.

PAPERBACK ISBN: 978-1-4166-0708-3   ASCD product #108013
Also available as an e-book through ebrary, netLibrary, and many online booksellers (see Books in Print for the ISBNs).

Quantity discounts for the paperback edition only: 10–49 copies, 10%; 50+ copies, 15%; for 1,000 or more copies, call 800-933-2723, ext. 5634, or 703-575-5634. For desk copies: member@ascd.org.

Library of Congress Cataloging-in-Publication Data

Burris, Carol Corbett.
   Detracking for excellence and equity / Carol Corbett Burris, Delia T. Garrity.
      p.   cm.
   Includes bibliographical references and index.
   ISBN 978-1-4166-0708-3 (pbk. : alk. paper) 1. Track system (Education)—United States. 2. Ability grouping in education—United States. 3. Slow learning children—Education--United States. 4. Academic achievement—United States. 5. Educational equalization—United States. I. Garrity, Delia T. II. Title.

   LB3061.8.B87 2008
   371.2′54—dc22

                                                                        2008014293

18 17 16 15 14 13 12 11 10 09 08   1 2 3 4 5 6 7 8 9 10 11 12

Detracking
for Excellence and Equity

Foreword

by Jeannie Oakes and Martin Lipton

There was a time when few policymakers, educators, or members of the public presumed that all school children could reach the same level of standards-based proficiency. Indeed, schools, districts, states, and the federal government promoted the idea that different children should strive for different levels of accomplishment. That has changed.

Today's standards-based education reforms and the No Child Left Behind act require all children to reach proficiency. Furthermore, official policies and rhetoric encourage the highest levels of achievement—going far beyond the lowest tolerable definitions of "proficiency." And yet, ability grouping and tracking remain robustly persistent in schools, even though no other schooling practice leaves children behind more systematically. The result is that countless children will not reach even the low proficiency thresholds many states have set.

In the face of standards-based reform, many but by no means all policymakers, researchers, and educators have proposed eliminating tracking. Such recommendations have been bolstered by research, including the Third International Mathematics and Science Study, which concluded in 1998 that tracking "fails to provide satisfactory achievement for either average or advanced students," and by research syntheses, such as that by the National Research Council in 1999 documenting strong negative effects of low-track classes (Heubert & Hauser, 1999; Schmidt, 1998). The evidence runs deep that tracking is rife with problems and that *detracking,* if allowed to proceed, is good for students. Nevertheless, educators, parents, and others have worried that there are no well-defined alternatives to tracked schools. At every turn, skeptics have warned that heterogeneous classes will either leave slower students behind or force quicker ones to wait. Less often acknowledged is a widespread fear that racial diversity in classrooms will have a negative impact on standards and rigor.

Carol Corbett Burris and Delia T. Garrity put such concerns to rest. Here in this book is evidence that heterogeneous grouping can foster high achievement and diminish racial and socioeconomic gaps. The detracking reform of the Rockville Centre School District resulted in the near-elimination of the district's racial achievement gap and South Side High School being named a U.S. Department of Education Blue Ribbon School of Excellence. In addition, the school is consistently listed as one of *Newsweek* magazine's "100 Best High Schools in the United States." What's more, the considerable gains made by lower-income African Americans were not won at the "expense" of students from groups that had achieved well under the old three-track system. The traditionally high-achieving students in this mostly affluent suburban community also succeeded at much higher rates than before detracking began. In 2004, the overall Regents diploma rate increased to a remarkable 94 percent, with 30 percent of the graduating class also earning an International Baccalaureate diploma.

This is first and foremost a practical book that shows how educators can make detracking work and provides evidence to back up the approach recommended. Burris and Garrity make the detracking process clear without trivializing the need for hard work and long-range commitment. They stress that success springs from providing all students access to a rich and challenging "accelerated" curriculum, and then map a course for doing that, with chapters full of useful guidelines and examples. And they show how school leaders can engage teachers in developing, implementing, and sustaining constructivist, multidimensional, and differentiated instruction; these are the practices found most often only in high-track classes or in schools in wealthy neighborhoods.

The authors also make it clear that detracking is more than a straight-forward curriculum reform or change in the school organization; it is the work of a career, not something to accomplish in the short term before moving on to the next challenge. Rockville Centre's detracking reform has taken years of steady and thoughtful work, with parallel attention to adults' and students' learning needs. The authors give due credit to the resources that allow them to support students who struggle academically, the well-qualified teaching staff, the school district's willingness to take risks, and parents who stood by the reform.

This support in the form of resources and people stemmed from a process more intricate than proffering a plainly described, research-supported good idea. The reform required careful cultural and political work. Those undertaking detracking must remain alert and watchful, aware of quickly arising challenges that are not lightly dismissed with evidence that school programs and organization are actually working for students.

The vigilance advocated in this book is both pragmatic and principled. The authors explain how detracking won't seem logical to either teachers or parents unless credible school leaders counter some deeply held cultural beliefs: that innate ability is more important than schooling, that only some students can benefit from accelerated instruction, and that the racial achievement gap is intractable. Challenges to these conventional beliefs must be brought into teachers' work as they revise the curriculum, design lessons, and develop assessments. Moreover, practices that challenge the conventions cannot be optional, but instead must be as inherent to the curriculum as subject-matter content. Far from being a "softer," more discretionary approach to instruction that some fear detracking will promote, the instructional timeline, designated content, and specified assessments are mandated.

Surely, the authors deserve our admiration and praise for their role in the astonishing accomplishments in Rockville Centre. But we think they deserve far more: recognition as examples for all educators and policymakers, who can follow their practical, realistic, and wise guidance and work toward improving education for all students.

Introduction

In September 1991, Ronnie entered South Side High School with the reputation of a struggling student. Not wanting to see Ronnie "frustrated" in college prep classes, his well-meaning counselor placed him in remedial reading and writing, general math, general science, and general social studies. The counselor also assumed that Ronnie would enjoy working with his hands, so wood shop was added to his program as an elective. The only Regents-level course* that Ronnie took was 9th grade Regents English.

The next year, Ronnie took general biology and consumer math—both courses represented the "low track"—as well as two college prep courses (Regents English and Regents social studies). However, when Ronnie failed the social studies course that year, he was demoted to the non-Regents track for both English and social studies in 11th grade, and he continued in low-track classes until he graduated. For this student, college prep was over.

Peter also entered South Side High School in 1991. Unlike Ronnie, who lived in the public housing project, Peter lived three blocks from the high school on an affluent avenue. In 9th grade he took Advanced Biology

---

*Regents courses are high school courses in New York State that follow a specified curriculum. Students take examinations at the end of each Regents course that, if passed, lead to a Regents diploma. The courses are generally regarded as college preparatory courses.

and Advanced Sequential II Mathematics, a geometry-based course. Because he had studied accelerated mathematics and science in the middle school, his senior year courses would include BC Calculus and International Baccalaureate (IB) Chemistry, Higher Level. While Ronnie pursued technology electives, Peter played in the school's woodwind ensemble. The two young men, who both attended the same middle school and lived in the same town, *may* have crossed paths in physical education classes, but they were unlikely to meet in any other class.

By September 2002, much had changed. In that year, Ronnie's neighbor, Tyrone, followed the same curriculum as Peter's next-door neighbor, Anna, including the 9th grade pre-IB English class. Because Tyrone's 8th grade test scores indicated that he would need academic assistance in English, he was assigned to a support class that met every other day. In the support class, his teacher worked with a small group of students to pre-teach and post-teach concepts from the challenging English 9 curriculum. Tyrone and Anna continued to follow this curriculum trajectory, and in 11th grade, both students took IB courses for English and history. Anna's elective courses were in art; Tyrone chose music. Both students declared themselves to be full International Baccalaureate diploma candidates in their junior year.

The advantages in the educational experiences of Tyrone over those of Ronnie are neither an example of extraordinary motivation nor the result of a gifted, young African American from a poor household having his talents uncovered by a caring mentor. They are not evidence of successful remediation, test prep, or improved preschool or reading programs. Rather, they are the result of a diverse suburban school district abandoning the practice of sorting and selecting students and choosing to put a rigorous curriculum in place for all students.

We believe that schools can improve if they are willing to re-examine and challenge traditional ideas about who should have access to the best curricula they offer. We believe that excellence and equity are compatible, and that schools that are willing to do the hard work of detracking with vigilance and care can effect remarkable improvements in learning for all students.

This book is intended to provide a guide for educators who are interested in understanding how schools can meet the challenge of providing both equity and excellence by eliminating the school-created structures that sort and select students, resulting in unequal educational opportunities. Throughout, we provide wisdom from our own experiences with tracking and detracking. We offer examples of the complexity of detracking reforms from the boardroom to the classroom, from meetings with teachers to meetings with parents. We share longitudinal data that demonstrate the efficacy of a detracking reform. Most important, we explain how schools can successfully undertake this complex reform that requires educators to examine and challenge their beliefs about intelligence, ability, and instruction. From our experiences as teachers, school leaders, and researchers, we have learned one simple truth: When a school community dismantles systems of educational stratification—whether they are called *tracking, ability grouping,* or *leveling*—remarkable benefits to students follow.

1
....

One District's Story

In 1986, South Side Middle School in suburban Rockville Centre, New York, was similar to many middle schools across the United States. Formerly a junior high school, it retained a tracked structure, with levels of courses from remedial to honors. These tracked classes, stratified by ethnicity and social class, did not reflect the demographic diversity of the school's student population. Upper middle class white students comprised the majority of students in high-track classes; ethnic minority students were, for the most part, in the low-track classes or in self-contained special education classes. There were five tracks in English and three each in social studies, science, and mathematics. Foreign language classes were not tracked, but taking a foreign language was reserved for the school's highest-achieving students, eliminating the need for a "lower" level of study for students who did not excel.

South Side Middle School's tracking system was particularly rigid in mathematics, with students carefully assigned to courses based on standardized test scores, grades, and teacher recommendations. Incoming 6th grade students needed to meet strict standards to qualify for a seat in one of the two sections of accelerated mathematics, the course of study that would lead to taking calculus in the senior year of high school. Even then, only the "Top 50" qualifying 6th graders were accepted, meaning that the "cut line" for admission to accelerated mathematics varied from year to year.

Tracking continued when students matriculated to South Side High School, which had a minimum of three tracks in addition to self-contained special education classes and an array of remedial and technology class electives. General education students were directed to "non-Regents" courses with unchallenging curricula. Other students were channeled into "Regents classes," the college prep course of study necessary to earn the New York State Regents diploma. Still others were selected for the "Regents with honors" track, taking rigorous honors classes that prepared them for Advanced Placement and International Baccalaureate (IB) courses in their senior year. Students' high school track assignment was determined almost exclusively by their middle school track placement. More often than not, well-meaning teachers recommended "borderline" students to a lower track rather than have them risk failure in a more rigorous curriculum. This practice not only prevented most students from attempting the top-tier IB diploma but also kept many students from pursuing the New York State Regents diploma designed to prepare them for college.

As was the case in the middle school, the demographics of each of the high school's tracked classes did not reflect the rich diversity of the student body in both family income and race. Although 9 percent of South Side High School's students were African American and 12 percent were Latino, 97 percent of the students in the highest track were white or Asian American students. And although the percentage of students who were eligible to receive free or reduced-price lunch ranged each year from 11 to 14 percent, it was unusual to find students from poor households in high-track classes.

Minority students and low-socioeconomic-status (SES) students were overrepresented in the lowest tracks, however. In addition, tensions existed between minority and majority students in the low-track classes, and the classroom focus was on discipline rather than academics. Learning outcomes reflected this inequity of opportunity. There were wide achievement gaps between the tracks that remedial and self-contained classes were never able to close. The more the curriculum was "slowed down," the wider the learning gap between high-track students and low-track students became.

In 1987, it became apparent to William H. Johnson, the new super-intendent of schools, that tracking was contributing to the gap in achieve-ment, and that the middle school was the critical point at which academic sorting began. Superintendent Johnson carefully examined the achieve-ment data for each of the middle school's demographic groups and noticed how the school was divided into the academic "haves" and "have-nots." This academic division closely mirrored the economic division in the dis-trict: students from wealthy homes were, for the most part, highly success-ful; students from homes with fewer financial resources were not doing as well; and students of color and poverty were meeting with little or no suc-cess in school.

Superintendent Johnson considered the divide to be unacceptable. Recognizing that low-track classes with low expectations were a major cause of the problem, he decided to do away with low-track classes. In 1989, the district's middle school English and social studies teachers started by redesigning the curriculum for grades 6–8 to follow an honors curriculum model. A few years later, in 1993, the superintendent set a clear, measurable goal: By the year 2000, 75 percent of all South Side High School students would earn a Regents diploma.

At that time, the district's Regents diploma rate—the number of stu-dents graduating with at least a Regents diploma—was 58 percent. To reach the 75-percent goal, the high school would need to give each student access to more challenging academic classes. The low-track, non-Regents courses would need to be eliminated. The effort to achieve this goal would need to span the grades from kindergarten through grade 12.

Detracking the Elementary Gifted Program

The five elementary schools in the district presented the first obstacle to detracking. Although there was no formal tracking system in place at that level, the gifted and talented program, which began in grade 4, tacitly fed the middle school honors track in academic subjects. The program had powerful parent advocates who lobbied for accelerated curricula and enrichment for their high-achieving students. The challenge for the district, then, was to ensure that gifted students had their needs met, while at the same time providing greater access for all students to the most challenging curricula of the middle and high school.

The solution was to transform the elementary gifted program from an exclusive program that served a few students to an inclusive program that identified and nurtured the gifts and talents of all students. Over a four-year period, the exclusive gifted and talented program was phased out as its curriculum was blended into each elementary classroom using a new district-wide enrichment program known as STELLAR, which stands for "Success in Technology, Enrichment, Library, Literacy, and Research." Staffing at each elementary building included (and still includes) a STELLAR teacher to support classroom teachers by enriching the grade-level curriculum.

Detracking the Middle School

As the transition in gifted education was taking place, administrators and teachers carefully dismantled the remnants of the middle school tracking system. The redesigned, detracked English and social studies program were operating well, with additional support classes set up in reading and writing to help students who struggled. The mathematics and science departments were more resistant to detracking, and in these subjects multiple tracks remained.

In 1990, middle-school tracking in mathematics and science decreased from three tracks to two, but there was still work to be done. South Side High School's principal, Robin Calitri, asked for the middle school's cooperation in preparing more students for the advanced mathematics and science courses required to achieve a Regents diploma. He was also interested in expanding the high school's International Baccalaureate program and increasing enrollment in Advanced Placement calculus courses. For this to happen, more 8th grade students would need to take the accelerated mathematics course called Sequential I Mathematics, then generally reserved for gifted 8th grade students statewide and, at South Side Middle School, restricted to the Top 50 qualifiers. Sequential I Mathematics culminated with a New York State Regents exam to measure student achievement. As expected, the middle school's restrictive enrollment policy translated into very high scores. Students' median score on the 8th grade Sequential I Mathematics Regents exam was 95 percent.

Principal Calitri found an ally in South Side Middle School's principal, Larry Vandewater, who readily agreed that more students should be allowed to take Sequential I Mathematics. He disagreed with the "limited seat" approach supported by the middle and high school mathematics departments and used the high school principal's request as well as Regents examination data as the rationale to open opportunity for more students.

Over the course of a few years, South Side Middle School revised its course assignment policy to remove restricted enrollment standards and allow students and parents to decide whether students would accelerate in mathematics. This paralleled the high school's movement toward open enrollment in honors and IB classes and the elimination of all low-track, non-Regents courses. Superintendent Johnson referred to the process as *leveling up* and strongly encouraged students to take the schools' most challenging courses. From 1992 until 1995, the number of middle school students opting to accelerate in mathematics grew from one-third to nearly one-half of the class. Yet the median score for 8th grade accelerated students on the Sequential I Regents exam remained high at 94 percent.

Although acceleration was now theoretically available to all students, in practice, white, African American, Asian, and Latino students were not choosing to accelerate at the same rates.* For example, during the 1996–1997 school year, only 11 percent of African American students and 15 percent of Latino students were accelerated in 8th grade mathematics, while the overall acceleration rate of white and Asian students was 50 percent. With the district's upper middle class students choosing to accelerate, the nonaccelerated pre-algebra 8th grade mathematics classes began to assume the characteristics of low-track classes documented in the literature on tracking (see Lucas, 1999; Oakes, 2005; Slavin & Braddock, 1993; Vanfossen, Jones, & Spade, 1987). Not only were minority students

---

*The phenomenon of students of color choosing lower-track classes in racially mixed schools is documented in a study by Yonezawa, Well, and Serena (2002), which we discuss briefly in Chapter 2.

overrepresented in the less demanding classes, failure rates in those classes were higher, and student motivation was lower.

The middle school assistant principal who supervised mathematics, coauthor Delia Garrity, studied the results of international reports such as the Third International Mathematics and Science Study (TIMSS), which demonstrated a connection between the underperformance of U.S. students and the repetitive and unchallenging math curricula of grades 6–8. She had observed that student performance had not decreased on the New York State Regents examination, even after the school had allowed more students to accelerate. She shared her findings with her colleagues, and school leaders began to consider a key question: If nearly half of all middle school students could successfully study accelerated math, why couldn't all students do so?

Based on the positive data from previous detracking efforts, the results of international studies, and the belief that all middle school students would benefit from instruction in high-level, heterogeneously grouped classes, the district developed a multiyear plan to eliminate all tracking in mathematics. After a careful review of the mathematics curriculum, teachers came to the conclusion that eliminating topic repetition would make it possible to compact the curricula of grades 6–8 into grades 6 and 7, teach the Sequential I Mathematics curriculum in grade 8, and accelerate all students in mathematics. Some teachers wanted the revised curriculum to begin in the elementary schools, which would have postponed acceleration at the middle school level for several years, but the middle school leadership team and the superintendent believed the delay was not necessary; thus, implementation began, despite teacher reservations, with the incoming 6th grade class of 1995. In June 1998, the first cohort of detracked, accelerated students took the New York State Sequential I Mathematics Regents examination in grade 8. The passing rate on the exam proved to be higher than passing rates obtained when students took the course in tracked middle and high school classes. Over 84 percent of the students passed the exam, and 52 percent attained mastery level (a score of 85 percent or above). That passing rate on the exam continued to improve in the two subsequent years.

Detracking the High School

As the middle school implemented detracking practices, the number of tracks in the high school decreased from three to two with the elimination of low-track, non-Regents classes. The first cohort of detracked students entered South Side High School in 1998 and chose either the Regents- or honors-level course of study in mathematics. Their middle school experience in detracked, accelerated math classes generated achievement benefits throughout their four years of high school (Burris, Heubert, & Levin, 2006). Over 50 percent of students went on to take an Advanced Placement calculus course in their senior year, and nearly all students passed the state examination in advanced algebra and trigonometry (the Sequential III Mathematics Regents examination) prior to graduation. Although the achievement gap in mathematics did not close, it narrowed dramatically. During the first three years following mathematics detracking, the percentage of minority students who passed the Sequential III Mathematics Regents exam increased from 46 percent to 67 percent.

Detracking did not end with mathematics in the middle school. After a review of the 9th grade English and social studies Regents and honors curricula, high school teacher leaders and administrators agreed to detrack 9th grade English and social studies classes beginning in September 1998. An "honors by application" process was retained to challenge high achievers during the first year, and in the second year of implementation (1999–2000), all students studied the former honors curriculum. Teachers noticed the improvement in performance of the students who would have taken the lower-track class. In addition, the heterogeneously grouped classes had fewer behavior problems than the former low-track classes and exhibited an academic tone similar to the former honors classes. Higher achievers were still challenged, and final examination results were good. In fact, the passing rates on the final examinations in English and social studies improved, even though the challenge level of the exams was similar to the former "honors" exams.

In 2000, New York unveiled new statewide curriculum standards for biology. South Side High School, needing to revise its biology curriculum to focus on these standards, took the opportunity to create one appropriate for a detracked, heterogeneous population. (The middle school had successfully detracked science, its last tracked subject, two years earlier.) Superintendent Johnson and the Board of Education approved the change to a single biology course, The Living Environment, for grade 9. At that point, mathematics was the only 9th grade subject that maintained two levels; the next year, the high school modified the already accelerated mathematics curriculum, begun in grade 8 and completed in grade 9, from a two-track course to one, heterogeneously grouped course titled Mathematics A. This course typically begins in grades 9 or 10 for most students in other New York state high schools.

Grade 10 was the next step in the detracking process. After discussion with school leaders and faculty, it was proposed that in September 2003, all 10th graders would take the same pre-IB English and social studies classes. Despite ample notice and data from the Sequential I Mathematics and Living Environment Regents exams demonstrating the success of detracking, some parents were furious. The principal and teachers carefully explained their rationale in public forums. Doubts remained for some, but the courses went forward and were highly successful. The passing rates in each course increased, teachers reported enjoying the academic tone of the classes, and parents, including many who had opposed the change, provided positive feedback. Perhaps most significantly, the number of minority students who elected to take IB English and history in 11th grade increased from 30 percent to 50 percent.

In September 2005, the high school detracked Mathematics B, an advanced, accelerated course. In 2006, it detracked chemistry. Each time a course was detracked, there was resistance from some parents. However, student achievement in these classes always increased by the end of the first year. For example, when Mathematics B classes detracked, the 10th grade passing rate on the Mathematics B Regents exam increased from 70 percent to 85 percent. This was a remarkable achievement, given that the State of New York considers Mathematics B to be an advanced mathematics course, and that most students who take the exam take it in grade 11.

Superintendent Johnson exceeded his goal for an increase in Regents diplomas. As a result of detracking, by 2000, the Regents diploma rate at

South Side High School was 84 percent, and it continued to rise in the years that followed. By 2005, it reached 97 percent. The achievement gap began closing as well. The overall rate of Regents diplomas had masked a considerable achievement gap between the district's majority and minority students. In 2000, only 32 percent of South Side High School's minority students achieved a Regents diploma; by 2005, that rate jumped to 92 percent. Detracking also benefited students with learning disabilities. From 2000 to 2005, the percent of special education students graduating with a Regents diploma increased dramatically, from 26 percent to 76 percent.

The effects of detracking went beyond the attainment of Regents diplomas. As detracking progressed, enrollment in the high school's IB program soared; over 80 percent of all members of the graduating class of 2007 took at least one IB course, and one-third of this graduating class earned the International Baccalaureate diploma. Ten years prior, in 1997, less than 30 percent of all graduates took at least one IB course, and just 6 percent of the class earned the IB diploma. Once the high school detracked, minority students' participation in the IB program increased dramatically as well. In 1999, only 6 percent of the school's minority students chose to pursue the rigorous IB course of study; in 2006, more than one-third of the school's minority students were IB diploma candidates.

Despite the expanded enrollment and greater heterogeneity of IB classes, South Side High school's IB examination scores have remained strong. The rate of students earning the highest scores on IB exams (6 and 7) has remained stable too, supporting the conclusion that greater heterogeneity does not necessarily result in a reduction of rigor, and that excellence need not come at the expense of equity (Burris, Welner, Wiley, & Murphy, 2007).

Examining the Detracking Reform

This chapter has presented an overview of what occurred as an integrated, suburban school district detracked. When tracks were dismantled, student achievement improved across the board, and the gaps between majority and minority students began to close. We share the story to demonstrate that detracking is not only possible, but can be clearly beneficial, especially for students who were underserved in low-track classes. The important message for educators, however, is found in both the results and the process of change.

As many who have attempted detracking know, it is far more than a mechanical process of dismantling low-track classes. It is a complex reform that requires educators, along with various members of the communities they serve, to examine and challenge their beliefs about intelligence, ability, and instruction. It takes political acumen, intense planning, and strong leadership. Those who attempt to detrack their schools encounter stiff resistance from groups who have a vested interest in the status quo and believe that their students or their children will be hurt by detracking (Oakes, 2005). Detracking requires teachers to examine their practices, learn new techniques, and change how they teach as the range of achievement levels in their classes widens. To sustain detracking reforms, educators must keep objective measures of students' learning and clearly communicate results with the community. And detracking requires a sense of mission grounded in the belief that public schools are democratic institutions dedicated to the success of all students, not just the academic elite.

Schools all over the United States are struggling to meet the mandates of the No Child Left Behind (NCLB) Act, which requires that *all* students meet high learning standards and that the gaps in achievement between racial and ethnic groups disappear. Although there is much to criticize about the mandate, it has forced schools to ask whether they are truly serving each student enrolled. The performance of a school's highest achievers will always be a source of pride, but their high achievement must not come at the expense of other students. Placing large numbers of students in low-track classes with inferior curricula will not prepare students for the assessments needed to demonstrate progress under NCLB, or more important, to be successful citizens in the 21st century. As long as a curriculum gap exists, so will an achievement gap.

Tracking, by its very nature, causes the achievement gap to widen. If one group of students is given an enriched and accelerated curriculum to study, and another group's learning is slowed down to a snail's pace by remediation, there can be no other outcome than a gap that widens over time. Providing all students access to the school's best curriculum, with support for those who struggle, gives students the opportunity to achieve based on high learning standards.

In the chapters to come, we share what we have learned through our involvement with the detracking of the Rockville Centre School District, including both our successes and our mistakes. In each chapter, we discuss the issues and challenges that must be addressed if a detracking reform is to be successful, and we explain the strategies we used. Whenever possible, we also interject what we have learned from the literature and from our colleagues. Although all schools and their contexts differ, we believe that there are overarching issues and principles that are worth sharing with those who wish to embark on this most important school reform, which can result in schools that are both excellent and equitable.

2

....

What Tracking Is and
How to Start Dismantling It

By the time the Rockville Centre School District began to examine its levels of courses, rigid educational systems—ones that formally assigned students to college prep, general, or vocational curricular paths or schools—had been largely dismantled in the United States and replaced with somewhat less rigid tracking systems characterized by curriculum differentiation. In modern tracking systems, students are assigned to different levels of the same course, or to a course with a different curriculum that is either more or less rigorous (Lucas, 1999; Oakes, 2005).

In some schools, tracking begins with kindergarten screening. IQ and early achievement tests designed to measure so-called "ability" determine track placement in the elementary years, thus setting in place an educational trajectory for 12 years of schooling. In other schools, tracking is a meritocracy that relies on teacher recommendations, grades, and student motivation to determine placement. In still others, students and their parents are allowed to choose a track, with certain conditions attached to the placement. A common example is allowing students to take an honors class provided that they maintain an average of 90 or above. Standards for track placement are uniform in some schools; in others, each department determines the number of tracks and track placement. For example, in the high school where one of the coauthors taught prior to coming to Rockville

Centre, any student was allowed to take AP English, but entrance to AP courses in foreign languages was determined by previous enrollment in the honors track and final averages in prior language courses.

Some tracking systems, referred to as *ability-grouping systems,* assign students to different classes based on their perceived ability in that subject. Still other tracking systems are called *leveling systems*—students, at least ostensibly, study the same curriculum, but they may need to first pass prerequisite courses (e.g., pre-algebra, pre-biology) or take the same course for a longer period. In a leveling system, a course might be taught to both high-achieving 8th graders and lower-achieving 10th graders. Or a course offered to most students in one period per day might be offered to students deemed "lower achievers" for two periods a day. Whatever the course's title or structure, grouping some students together and requiring them to take that course apart from other students is a form of tracking (Oakes, 2005).

Key Questions for Getting Started

Schools that want to dismantle their tracking system should begin by analyzing grouping practices in their school and district, regardless of the label used by the district. This analysis should focus on the long-term effects of the school's grouping practices. When South Side Middle School began the process of dismantling tracking in mathematics, it was because the school leaders recognized the deleterious effect that tracking in mathematics had on a student's ability to earn a Regents or International Baccalaureate diploma. It became apparent that the effects of tracking in the middle school extended far beyond 8th grade.

An examination of the present system in a school or district begins with asking and answering these questions:

1. At what grade level are students first grouped for instruction?
2. What is the rationale for starting to group at that grade level, and how many grouping levels are used?
3. What influence does this grouping have on students' later instructional placement and educational opportunities?

4. What assessments are the basis for placement decisions?
5. How accurate and valid are these placement assessments?
6. How are the effectiveness of placement decisions assessed?

The conversations spawned by these questions will help colleagues reflect on and communicate their beliefs about intelligence and the purpose of schooling. Some faculty members will question whether tracking allows all students an equal opportunity to take the school's best courses; others will believe that placing students in courses matched to their ability is an important obligation of schooling. Some teachers will believe that their instructional skills and manner of delivery play an important role in student achievement; others will see instructional issues as tangential and secondary to innate ability or student motivation.

During the detracking process in our school district, we listened carefully to the language that teachers used in those conversations to learn which of our colleagues would be on board and which would be resistant. Helping teachers (and parents) explore their beliefs is an ongoing and important process. Often we discover that our assumptions may not be supported by data, or that there are long-term ramifications to tracking that we had not previously understood. There is an additional benefit to these conversations. As with any other school reform, a detracking initiative can't be put on hold until everyone believes in it. There will always be some who will object to a new way of doing things. Early conversations can identify a cadre of teachers who are open to the idea of teaching heterogeneous classes. In addition, such conversations can help a faculty understand the belief systems that influence teachers' day-to-day interactions with students.

Belief Systems That Sustain Tracking

Language can be very revealing. Teachers talk about their "low" kids, their "advanced" kids, their "regular" kids, and their "overachievers." On an online message board for New York State chemistry teachers, one member had this to say:

The Regents kids of today are just a touch above our general level kids of a decade ago. Then I have the other kids who are nice kids and get decent grades, but are WAY behind the top kids. Gads, I love my period 1 and 4 honors chem classes!!!! They are some of the best kids I have ever had the honor of teaching. (ChemBond Listserv, April 2006)

Notice all the labels this teacher assigns to students: *Regents kids, general kids, top kids, honors kids, best kids.* If your child attended this teacher's school, which designation would you want him or her to receive? How might the teacher's labeling constructs affect day-to-day interactions with students? For which class is this teacher probably putting forth the greatest teaching effort?

As our school district began its detracking reform, we began to pay attention to our language. Language shapes our thinking and our beliefs. We began with the word "ability" and made a conscious effort to replace it with "achievement." Thus, we write about, study, and talk about students who are lower achievers or higher achievers. *Achievement* is a measurable construct that describes what a student knows at a given point in time; *ability* implies an innate quality that cannot change and that limits success. As we made this commitment personally, we shared it with our faculty. Our language began to change, and so did the way we viewed students. Discussions about the labels placed on students and the beliefs they represent can help a faculty that is embarking on a detracking reform question constructs and practices that they have taken for granted. Being conscious of our own language can help us understand how deeply ingrained the culture of student sorting is. Language awareness is also likely to help uncover other justifications for tracking.

Perhaps the most accurate description of the belief systems that sustain tracking comes from Jeannie Oakes and Martin Lipton. In their 1999 essay "Access to Knowledge: Challenging the Techniques, Norms, and Politics of Schooling," Oakes and Lipton discuss how the categories that human beings create to explain differences in children change from school-created labels of differences to reified "realities" that limit opportunities for learning:

Those who promote ability grouping, special education, gifted programs, and the myriad other homogeneous instructional groups in schools claim that these classifications are objective and color blind, rather than, as Goodlad suggests, reflecting myths and prejudices. Advocates of grouping explain the disproportionate classification of white students as gifted or advanced and of students of color as slow or basic as the unfortunate consequence of different backgrounds and abilities. They base their claims of objectivity on century-old (and older) explanations of differences that are neither scientific nor bias-free.

Both students and adults mistake labels such as "gifted," "honors student," "average," "remedial," "LD" and "MMR" for certification of overall ability or worth. These labels teach students that if the school does not identify them as capable in earlier grades, they should not expect to do well later. Everyone without the "gifted" label has the de facto label of "not gifted." The resource classroom is a low status place and students who go there are low status students. The result of all this is that most students have needlessly low self-concepts and schools have low expectations. Few students or teachers can defy those identities and expectations. These labeling effects permeate the entire school and social culture. (p. 171)

Do students differ in talents and achievement? They do. But when those observed differences are reinforced by track placement and grouping practices, and children then internalize those differences, learning opportunities become limited for all but the elite student. The talents of late bloomers go undiscovered, and the rewards of hard work and diligent study are never realized.

Here are some key questions about belief systems to discuss with colleagues:

1. What is human intelligence?

2. Is intelligence one-dimensional or multidimensional?

3. Which is more important to successful learning—aptitude or hard work?

4. Is it possible to make lessons more accessible to all students?

5. Is it possible for students to show what they know in a variety of ways?

6. If teachers' own children were to attend a tracked school, which track would they want them to be in and why?

Data and Detracking

The process of reassessing one's beliefs is a difficult one. It's even more difficult to persuade others to reassess their beliefs and, together, come to consensus on a new course of action. Too often educators find themselves stuck in intractable positions, unable to make progress on important issues due to disagreements.

Using data as a focal point for pedagogical discussion is a powerful way to help a school faculty and community begin to understand the deleterious effects of tracking. Focusing on data may result in the cognitive dissonance that will set doubters on the path to changing their beliefs. It also grounds early conversations in fact rather than opinion. Everyone has an opinion about tracking based on personal beliefs about human learning capacity and intelligence. These beliefs are often peppered by one's own experiences, vested interests, and at times, prejudices. In our district, whenever we focused discussions on data, participants began to be able to look at tracking in a more objective manner. Although a focus on data will not inoculate against controversy, it can help open discussions and minds.

Student Transcripts

One way to begin to assess the effects of tracking is to examine student transcripts. After carefully blocking any identifiable student information, such as names and addresses, transcripts can be used to compare the grades, standardized test scores, and course-taking patterns of students in high-track and low-track classes. When we examined transcripts from our schools, we noticed patterns that told us a lot about the trajectories that students were placed on by tracking; for instance, we learned about Ronnie and Peter, whom you met in the Introduction. Although we had been telling parents and students that it was possible for students to move to higher track classes after beginning in the lower tracks, we found no evidence that this upward movement was in fact taking place. Instead, the opposite was happening—it was not uncommon for students to move from the middle track to the lowest track.

The propensity for middle-track students to move to lower tracks rather than higher tracks during their high school years is not unique to our district. In his book *Tracking Inequality*, Samuel Lucas (1999) uses national test data to demonstrate that track movement occurs in a downward direction far more frequently than it does in an upward direction. Often, when faculty and parents see how dramatically different educational experiences can be from the high track to the low track, a healthy sense of social justice enters the conversation. In addition, it is always interesting to look at grades after the downward movement has occurred. Grades often fail to improve, even though the curriculum is easier.

Achievement and Track Placement

Proponents of tracking assume that tracking is fair. They believe that when school personnel decide to place students in different classes, there is wisdom, based on objective data, supporting these decisions. This is a very important assumption to verify, because the decision to deny students access to high-track courses, such as AP or IB courses, will affect their candidacy to competitive colleges.

When coauthor Carol Corbett Burris (2003) studied the effects of detracking mathematics in the middle school as the focus of her doctoral dissertation, she was shocked to discover how many high-achieving minority students did not study accelerated math prior to detracking, and how many majority students with far lower achievement test scores did so successfully. Again, these findings are not unique. The inequity and inefficiency associated with track placement are well documented in both national and international studies.

The Second International Mathematics Study (SIMS) was a comprehensive survey of mathematics taught and learned around the world. Twenty-two nations participated in this broad and longitudinal study that took place from 1976 to 1989. SIMS researchers Kifer, Wolfe, and Schmidt (1993) identified four levels of 8th grade math study typically found in most American middle or junior high schools, which they termed *remedial, regular, enriched,* and *algebra.**

For the SIMS study, 8th graders in all four tracks completed a pretest of pre-algebra arithmetic skills at the beginning of the year. Researchers examined the distribution of scores on the test by student and by math track. Although it was expected that class-type performance would be different, Kifer and colleagues' (1993) analysis of student and classroom performance found considerable score overlap among tracks.

Only half of the students who achieved the top 10 scores on the pretest and one-third of the students in the top 25 had actually been placed in the algebra-level classes. Inequities existed on the other end of the proficiency spectrum as well: Nearly 50 percent of the students assigned to remedial classes had scores that were better than 25 percent of the students in general math. In addition, Kifer and colleagues found that 5 of the 23 remedial classes had higher mean scores than 75 percent of the students in general math, 50 percent of the students in pre-algebra, and 25 percent of the students in algebra.

Welner (2001) found a similar pattern in his extensive study of San Jose, California, schools in the process of detracking: There was a vast overlap in prior achievement across all tracks in all of the schools studied. During Welner's study, he discovered that tracked classes were far from homogeneous in either ability or skill. Although mean scores were different, the overlap in the range of scores was remarkable.

These examples illustrate that the basic objective of tracking—the formation of homogenous classes with relation to skill and prior achievement—is rarely realized. Tracking does not create classes in which students are alike. The studies also illustrate that students of lower achievement are often placed in high-track classes, either accidentally or by design. What is of greatest interest is that when this happens, the formerly lower-achieving

---

*A recent study of curriculum based on TIMSS found six levels of study: the four found in SIMS plus enriched math and pre-algebra (Cogan, Schmidt, & Wiley, 2001).

students are often more successful. For example, one study of the effects of tracking in mathematics found that if lower-achieving students were mistakenly placed in the high-track mathematics class, their chances of successfully completing a college prep course of math study dramatically increased (White, Gamoran, Porter, & Smithson, 1996). This phenomenon has certainly been borne out in our own experience with accelerating all students (Burris et al., 2006).

Strategies for Beginning

Once you've made the decision to begin the detracking process in your school or district, you'll need to make a plan. The strategies that follow will assist in creating a blueprint for successful curriculum integration for all students.

Engage in Thoughtful Study

Detracking needs to begin with a conversation that questions the status quo. Sometimes this conversation takes place among school leaders; at other times it is a conversation among teachers or other stakeholders. We once gave information and guidance to a group of parents in Montgomery County, Maryland, who were anxious to begin a detracking reform. Although the educational roles of those who challenge tracking may differ from school to school, advocates of detracking share a common belief that the status quo is not serving the needs of all students, and thus they are anxious to advocate for change. Once the conversation begins, however, supporters of tracking are highly likely to become defensive. We recommend that those who want to create more equitable schools become familiar with facts that will help them focus emotionally charged conversations on data rather than opinion.

A good place to start is with studies such as those discussed in the previous section, along with others that identify the factors that influence track placement, from class size to parent pressure (see Hallinan, 1992; Useem, 1992a, 1992b). Summarize and discuss these studies and their implications with your colleagues. When Delia Garrity began talking about detracking middle-school mathematics, she grounded her statements in the results of the TIMSS study, which showed that 8th graders around the globe were successfully taking algebra. Next, take a look at your school data. We suggest that you analyze data in a manner similar to the studies described above. Use objective data from a standardized test as your measure of prior student achievement, and then record which track students were placed in both initially and later in their schooling. When our district analyzed middle-school track placement data, we used scores on an elementary standardized assessment, the Iowa Tests of Basic Skills. If you are analyzing high school data, 10th grade PSAT scores are a good source of objective achievement data that correlate strongly with measures of general intelligence (Frey & Detterman, 2004). You will be surprised by how heterogeneous each of your courses already is. To capture the effect, be sure to look at the range of scores (see Welner, 2001), not just mean scores.

This hidden heterogeneity can become a powerful argument in favor of the elimination or reduction of tracking. If some lower achievers are already doing well in high-track classes, why can't more students have the same access? And if some higher achievers are assigned to low-track classes, what does that say about the efficacy and equity of the system?

Now go one step further by disaggregating data by ethnicity, socioeconomic status, and special education designation. This process will reveal how your school's achievement gaps correlate with tracks. Once you combine the data you've compiled with the answers to the questions in the previous section, you are prepared to engage in serious discussions about how to improve your school or district.

Using administrative fiat to completely remove all tracks in one fell swoop will fail to adequately prepare students, faculty, or parents for this complex reform. On the other hand, it is easy to fall into the trap of "getting ready to get ready to get ready," thereby delaying implementation until far into the future. Steps must be taken to move the process along. The next three strategies are the ones that we used simultaneously over the course of several years to implement and expand the reform in our district.

Begin Where Tracking Starts

Detracking should begin where tracking begins. If your elementary school tracks, that is the place to start. If tracking is delayed until the middle school years, begin there.

In our district, we encountered some resistant teachers who wanted to start by changing the curriculum in the elementary schools, even though there was no grouping for instruction at the elementary level. However, Superintendent Johnson wisely recognized that the true agenda of delay was overall resistance to the reform. He identified the critical beginning of mathematics tracking in grade 6 and determined that was the place to begin detracking. Therefore, we implemented accelerated math in hetero-geneous classes in 6th grade, and then followed that with the next year's 7th and then 8th grade programs, moving with the student cohort.

We carefully collected, analyzed, and communicated data each step of the way in order to provide continued impetus to move forward. Com-paring the passing rates and grades of the students in the detracked cohorts with students in tracked cohorts made it clear that the students were doing better in the heterogeneously grouped classes than tracked students had done in past years. These data provided an objective coun-terbalance to those teachers who felt that the acceleration of all students was not working.

Begin with Teachers Who Are Interested

It is not an accident that our detracking began in both the district's middle and high school with the English and social studies departments. In both cases, these departments were the most open to the idea of heterogeneous grouping and the most able to envision all students learning the high-track curriculum. When we began special education inclusion in the mid-dle and high school, we began with volunteers. This is not to say that *all* teachers in these departments were wholeheartedly on board, or that this reform would have come spontaneously from these departments. In both cases, however, there was a core group of teachers who were willing to embrace the reform and had a natural understanding of the disadvantages of tracking. For those teachers who taught both high and low tracks, the disadvantages of tracking were easier to see.

Similarly, interested teachers led a detracking reform at East High School in Denver, Colorado. The school began detracking using a voluntary system created by two English teachers who were appalled by the nonacademic culture of their low-track classes (Yettick, 2006). They were supported in their efforts by their principal and University of Colorado at Boulder professors Kevin Welner and Ed Wiley. Grade 9 students at East High were placed in either a heterogeneously grouped English class, which studied an accelerated (high-track) curriculum, or a traditional tracked class. Parents were allowed to remove their child from the detracked class if they wished. Despite initial worries, none chose to do so. The experiment was a success, both academically and socially, for the students in the heterogeneous, accelerated classes. East High expanded the program the following year and added support classes for struggling students in the detracked sections. The efforts of just a handful of thoughtful, innovative teachers can jumpstart detracking in your school.

Finally, the impetus for detracking can emanate from national policy. Such was the case in Finland. The decision to detrack, and its beneficial effects on student achievement, are described in Figure 2.1.

Eliminate the Lowest Track First

There is little doubt that tracking does the most harm to students who are consigned to the lowest track. According to the National Research Council (NRC), low-track classes have an especially deleterious effect on learning, since such classes are "typically characterized by an exclusive focus on basic skills, low expectations, and the least qualified teachers" (Heubert & Hauser, 1999, p. 282). Placement in a low-track class is often used as a solution for student misbehavior or inattentiveness. The preponderance of research regarding low-track classes was so overwhelmingly negative that the NRC concluded that students should not be educated in low-track classes as they are currently designed (Heubert & Hauser, 1999). It makes sense, therefore, to begin by eliminating the classes that do the most harm to students. When our high school began the first phase of detracking, the low-track classes were the first to go.

You should be prepared for opposition to phasing out low-track classes. Many have argued that these classes should not be eliminated but

FIGURE 2.1

Nationwide Detracking: The Schools of Finland Close the Gap

In 2000, the 15-year-olds of Finland proved themselves to be among the best readers in the world, as measured by their performance on the Program for International Student Assessment (PISA), an internationally standardized assessment of the learning of 15-year-old students jointly developed by participating countries. In 2003, Finnish teenagers were first not only in reading, but also in mathematical literacy, problem solving, and science when compared with the students of 29 participating industrialized nations, including the United States, Hong Kong, and Korea (BBC News, 2004). In addition, Finland's gap between high and low achievers was the second smallest among the participating industrialized nations in 2000, and the smallest in 2003 (Cavanagh, 2005; Linnakyla & Valijarvi, 2005). Finally, the socioeconomic status (SES) of Finnish families has little impact on the achievement of Finnish students, when compared with the SES impact in other nations (Linnakyla & Valijarvi, 2005). While there are many possible factors that may contribute to the success of Finnish students, one of the most remarkable features of the national school system is its commitment to a unified school system with no tracking until students reach age 16 (Coughlan, 2004).

Other features of Finland's schools include the following:

• All students are entitled to the same high-quality education regardless of their prior achievement, gender, ethnicity, or social class (Finnish National Board of Education, 2004).

• "Ability grouping" in grades 1–9 was abolished in 1985 so that all could be eligible for higher education (Finnish National Board of Education, 2004).

• Special education students are included in regular classrooms (Linnakyla & Valijarvi, 2005).

• The Finnish system of basic education has a philosophy of teaching that "school is for every child, and that the school must adjust to the needs of every child, not the other way around" (Linnakyla & Valijarvi, 2005, p. 35).

• There is a national curriculum with school and teacher flexibility. Instruction is student-centered, and there is ample support for struggling students (Linnakyla & Valijarvi, 2005).

reformed instead: provided with better curriculum, better strategies, and additional time. In our opinion, successful reform of low-track classes is highly unlikely. By way of illustration, we share the following anecdote.

During our first year of middle school math acceleration, it was discovered that some of the special education inclusion students had not been adequately prepared for the Regents exam in the middle school because their teacher felt that the course was "too difficult" for them. These students would need to take the course over again in high school. Rather than fold them into heterogeneously grouped classes with new entrants to the school system who had not taken accelerated mathematics, as 9th graders, the special education inclusion students were assigned to a class of their own: a double-period class with extra resources. The class was small (fewer than 15 students), and three excellent, committed educators—a math teacher, a special education teacher, and a teaching assistant—were assigned to teach it. The class followed the New York State Regents curriculum. Other students, identified by counselors as "low achievers," were assigned to this class as well.

The idea was a serious mistake. The class culture was not academic, the students behaved disruptively, and the double-period schedule proved to be torture for both them and the teachers. In an effort to save the class, the most disruptive students were taken out and placed in the heterogeneously grouped class. This led to better behavior and academic performance from the previously disruptive students, but back in the special low-track class, another student would invariably take on the role as the lead disruptor. Needless to say, we never pursued a tracked solution again. Today, all special education students fully participate in the accelerated course, and teachers do not make their own decisions regarding students' capabilities.

Mary T. Fletcher, one of South Side Middle School's special education teachers, has taught in both self-contained and inclusion settings in elementary and middle school, and she has seen the positive changes heterogeneous classes bring to all students. She believes that providing differentiated instruction in a heterogeneous class enhances each student's academic, social, and emotional learning experience. She shares the story of how one student benefited from a heterogeneous classroom:

> Cathy was an 8th grade transfer student who worked diligently at earning and maintaining her "big bad bully" persona. She was so effective that peers and staff alike were frightened of her. Fortunately, Cathy joined a heterogeneous English classroom that implemented differentiated instruction.

During a unit on nonfiction, Cathy chose to create a visual of the destructive power of a forest fire in response to the literary image of a dragon's tongue of devouring flames. This became Cathy's hook. She painstakingly created a beautiful and haunting depiction of a dragon blotting out the sky and reducing a mighty forest to a collection of spindly sticks. The class and teacher were awed by her work. For the first time, Cathy was absorbed in completing an assignment. She worked on it after school, at home, and during free periods. Her peers and teachers saw a new side of Cathy, and she received positive attention for her newly revealed talents. In addition, her poster deepened the class's conversation about the piece, benefiting the high-achieving students in the class. The metaphor was closely examined, and Cathy's work became a conversation with the text, reflecting and contributing to the class's understanding of the essay.

Cathy's story provides some examples of how a heterogeneous classroom can improve the quality of education for all students. According to Mary Fletcher, there are many benefits to expect when instructional staff are conversant with and dedicated to differentiated instruction and detracking:

• *Teachers get to know their students better.* As teachers work to differentiate the curriculum, they develop an awareness and understanding of their students as learners.

• *Students feel respected and cared for by teachers who make the effort to reach them by developing careful, differentiated lesson plans.* Such students become assured that their classroom is a safe learning environment.

• *Differentiation allows more students to feel invested in the lesson, thereby decreasing behavioral problems.* Students who previously opted to be viewed as "bad" rather than "stupid" will have their learning needs met and other talents explored, allowing them to drop the "bad" act and become instead a valuable member of the class.

• *Students who might have been considered less intelligent because they learn in a nontraditional way become invaluable contributors to the heterogeneous classroom.* For example, an aural learner who struggles with textbook assignments can add in-depth perspective in a social studies class discussion by contributing what he or she has learned through documentaries or tapes.

• *Struggling students who are part of heterogeneous groups and classrooms observe and learn the techniques of less-inhibited learners.* They begin to see that "smart kids" don't always know the answers, have to pause to think, and use questions to orient themselves. Students in low-track classes are cut off from exposure to the habits of successful learners.

• *Differentiated instruction encourages flexibility.* Teachers thus become adept at adapting lessons to fulfill each student's individual needs.

• *Detracking removes the limits that come with rigid thinking about how learning should and does occur.* Fair does not always mean "the same." For example, allowing a student who struggles with the physical act of writing to type his notes can benefit that student and the rest of the class. Not only does the student get access to the material, but the entire class has a reliable set of notes that can be used for those who were absent. This student now becomes an expert—and essential—note-taker who takes pride in his responsibility and sees himself as a member of the class.

Opening the Gates Through Choice

During the first phase of detracking in our school district, we reduced the number of high school tracks from three to two, phasing out the lowest track. At the same time, the district opened enrollment in honors courses, the higher of the two tracks. Students were allowed to enroll in honors courses in grades 9 and 10, and IB and AP courses (the honors courses) in grades 11 and 12. Teachers and counselors still made placement recommendations, but parents and students made the decision. A similar process was followed in the middle school prior to the mathematics acceleration of all students.

There were several advantages to this approach. First, it allowed parents who were worried about the influx of the former "low-track" students into the middle track to move their children up to the honors track. Although this is a less-than-noble reason for opening access to the high track, it did quell some parent opposition and allowed the reform to proceed politically. More important, this approach demonstrated that far more students could study the school's most challenging curriculum with great success. Students felt more in charge of their educational destiny.

Counselors no longer needed to defend teacher recommendations that excluded students from taking the high-track classes in which they were interested. And most important of all, teachers adjusted to greater heterogeneity in honors, IB, and AP classes. Teaching strategies changed so that less time was spent on lecture and more time was spent on activities that engaged students in learning. Alternative ways to present concepts became the norm. Extra help became more important. The academic climate of the school "leveled up." All of the above helped smooth the way for the heterogeneous grouping to come, as the two tracks became a single enriched course for all students.

It is important, however, to stress that this type of two-track open enrollment should never be the final outcome, especially at the middle school and beginning high school levels. Our open enrollment process resulted in some stratification associated with the choice, counteracting the intent of the detracking process. We recommend that if you have a choice system, make the high track the default track and allow parents and students to opt out if they so desire. This approach should alleviate some of the problems we encountered. For a fuller discussion of the limitations of choice, we recommend an excellent research study on the topic: "Choosing Tracks: 'Freedom of Choice' in Detracking Schools" (Yonezawa, Wells, & Serena, 2002).

No matter how and where you begin, however, you cannot achieve long-term success without making a commitment to the development of a strong curriculum that preserves high standards for student learning. Placing all students in the same class and then allowing teachers to "teach to the middle" will result in a short-lived reform that is not in the best interest of all students. Chapter 3 will discuss what we have learned about developing an enriched curriculum that challenges and supports all learners.

3

....

The Curriculum Process
for Leveling-Up Instruction

As you may have surmised, we believe that there is no justification for offering some students an inferior curriculum. Students in low-track classes fall farther and farther behind, experiencing no remediation at all (Kerckhoff, 1986). The reality is that you can't close the achievement gap until you close the curriculum gap that is created by tracking. We have learned from experience that when teachers teach the same high-level rigorous curriculum to all students, the achievement gap narrows.

The careful revision and implementation of curriculum, then, is key to the success of a detracking reform. Unfortunately, many schools seem not to take curriculum seriously—why else would so many curriculum documents sit on shelves gathering dust? Too often an individual teacher or a team of teachers design and produce a curriculum with little or no input from administrators or colleagues, and as a consequence, colleagues continue to employ their own curriculum sequence, use their own instructional resources, and administer their own assessments, as if the new curriculum did not exist. In other cases, a new textbook becomes the curriculum, rather than serving as a resource used to implement the curriculum. Finally, administrators frequently provide only minimal guidance to teachers in terms of academic expectations, the structure of curriculum documents, and final review before publication.

The Curriculum Revision Process

If detracking is to be successful, careful curricular revisions are essential. The curriculum in detracked classrooms must be enriched and must provide teachers with opportunities to focus on the processes, as well as the products, of learning. Three components must be in place for successful implementation of a new curriculum: (1) teacher buy-in throughout the change process; (2) structured professional time for teachers to work on the implementation; and (3) close monitoring of the implementation by supervisors.

Teacher Buy-In

A solution commonly used to address the problem of students struggling with academic curriculum is to place them either in separate classes that stretch the same curriculum over two or more years or to place them in multiple periods of instruction. Many educators believe that these two scenarios are equally effective and that the regular curriculum is provided, only at a slower pace, thus giving all students equal educational opportunities. This is not true, however. While on paper each curriculum may include the same topics, and all students may sit for the same external assessment at the end of the course, the similarities end there. The reality is that the level of instruction, the quality of class discussions, and the depth of student understanding vary greatly in each scenario. Curriculum comes to life in a classroom as students and teachers construct meaning from what is taught.

As discussed in Chapter 2, South Side High School's attempt at stretching a course for a group of low-achieving students over two years did not work. Detracking proved that such a solution is far less effective than placing students in heterogeneous classes with high student expectations (see Burris et al., 2006). This is because track placement affects teachers' expectations for students. Teachers believe that students in higher-track classes are capable of participating in higher-level discussions, analyzing more complex material, and synthesizing information from various sources. On the other hand, teachers often assume that students in the slower-paced class are best served with simplistic explanations of topics, teacher-directed lessons, and rote memorization of content (Oakes, 2005).

Students quickly acclimate to their teachers' assumptions and expectations (Weinstein, 2002). Students in low-track classes internalize the beliefs that they are not good students and that school is a place where they will meet with little success. The culture of such classes becomes non-academic, and excessive time is spent on behavior management issues. Regardless of the type of curriculum implemented, the best intentions quickly disappear in a downward spiral.

To change the mind-set of those who believe in the effectiveness of low-track classes, we suggest that you start with an examination of the data. Data are objective and speak loud and clear. To ensure reliability, analyze data from assessments that are external, rather than teacher-created. Are assessment scores from a two-year course comparable to the scores from a one-year class? Try to find students who have similar prior achievement scores but were placed in different tracks. Chances are you will find, as we did, that the slower pace of instruction brought little, if any, increase in test scores.

Look beyond the pass/fail percentages and disaggregate data by race, socioeconomic status, and special education designation. We suggest that you begin with the following questions:

1. When are students taking the final assessments for a course? Are some students taking an exam after one year of instruction while others take the same exam after a year and a half or two years of instruction? Are some students taking three or more years to pass a two-year course due to failure along the way? Are there patterns of race or socioeconomic status?

2. What later educational opportunities are denied students in the lower track?

3. Who is passing? Examine the demographics of the data by race/ethnicity, socioeconomic status, and special education designation.

4. Compare the high school transcript of a student who participated in an honors course with that of a peer who did not. Are the two students equally prepared for college? Is there equity in their education?

Although teachers will grasp the implications of the data, not all will agree that all students are capable of passing a rigorous, honors-level course. Dissenters will offer a multitude of reasons why an "honors for all" or "leveling-up" approach will harm rather than help students. Some will worry that low-achieving students will encounter self-esteem issues if they struggle with a higher-level course. Some will be concerned that high-achieving students will suffer because the teacher will "teach to the middle" and not be able to provide rich educational experiences for the former high-track student. Instead of dismissing such worries out of hand, discuss them within the context of problem solving. Solutions may include the development of curricula for support classes for struggling students and extension activities for high achievers. Instructional leadership is critical at this point. The development of clear, concise, mandated curricula is the first step toward successful detracking.

Structured Professional Time for Curriculum Development

In our district, we employ a multistep process for curriculum design and revision. Once the administrative team at the building and central office, with the blessing of the Board of Education, determines that all students will, for example, study an honors curriculum in a specific course, or participate in the elementary gifted program, teachers take part in curriculum and course design. At the secondary level, the assistant superintendent for curriculum and teachers of both the honors curriculum and the lower tracks meet for a full day of professional development to begin the process of curriculum upgrading. If necessary, an outside consultant joins the team. Our district used an adapted form of the backward design process articulated in *Understanding by Design* by Grant Wiggins and Jay McTighe (2005) to develop our curriculum. Our curriculum planner, designed by literacy consultant Dale Worsley (Worsley, Fox, Landzberg, & Papagiotas, 2003), begins with the desired result and works backwards: all curriculum goals and objectives target the desired result. The curriculum planner is dynamic in that its components continually expand from general to more specific ideas and concepts. It provides a structure for initial conversation, a reality check for tangential conversation, and a final assessment of the completed curriculum. The curriculum planner helps teachers identify core beliefs, local and external mandates, vital understandings, essential questions, skills, fundamental knowledge, instructional strategies, resources, external and internal assessments, and a timeline for implementation.

During the process of curriculum design, teachers must be allowed to openly express their concerns, burning questions, and non-negotiables. It is essential that each professional lay his or her cards on the table. Each teacher brings a level of expertise as well as a perspective on how a course or program should be taught, and everyone must feel that these components will be part of the discussion. Teachers support the implementation of the curriculum when they believe that their voices are respected and truly part of the dialog. The collective wisdom of the group enhances the final product, as it reflects a synthesis of the best practices and instructional beliefs of the individuals.

STELLAR: An Inclusive Gifted Program for Grades K–5

The inclusive gifted program put in place in our district at the elementary level is called STELLAR, which stands for Success in Technology, Enrichment, Library, Literacy, and Research. The STELLAR curriculum was researched and designed by the assistant superintendent for curriculum, the elementary principals, and a team of teachers that included the gifted teacher, the enrichment teacher, elementary library/media specialists, and classroom teachers. Working with the philosophy that all students have gifts and talents, the team structured the curriculum using Renzulli's schoolwide enrichment model (Renzulli & Reis, 1997), Gardner's theory of multiple intelligences, (1993), and Bloom's taxonomy (1956). After attending a summer symposium on Renzulli's model, the teaching team adapted it to address the district's goals for all students in grades K through 5.

The heart of the STELLAR program is the elementary curriculum. Each STELLAR activity extends the curriculum with creative, challenging enrichment opportunities for all students, incorporating library, computer, and research skills when appropriate. The design team brought many talents to this project based on their collective professional experiences.

During the initial planning in the summer of 1999, the team examined New York's state standards in English, social studies, library research, science, and mathematics, as well as the district's curriculum, to look for opportunities to develop extension activities. The overarching goal of inspiring gifted behaviors in all students through the development of critical thinking skills guided their work. The teachers designed common districtwide extensions but left ample time for individual classroom and building initiatives. The curriculum team drew from Renzulli's schoolwide enrichment model (Renzulli, 1994; Renzulli & Reis, 1997), which includes three types of enrichment levels: Type I, general exploratory activities that expose children to an array of experiences beyond the classroom via visiting speakers, authors, and artists; Type II, group activities that include the development of critical thinking skills, research skills, and written, oral, and visual communication skills; and Type III, individual and small-group experiences that provide opportunities for advanced study and research in an area of interest.

At the district level, the STELLAR teachers planned a 2nd grade Type II activity called "Artifact Boxes" to enrich and extend students' study of individual states in the United States. This commercially produced unit, which can be found at www.artifactbox.com, links each class to a class in a state other than New York. Each class creates an artifact box that includes items that represent their state and their town. Students have to research, for example, the history, economy, environment, and culture of their geographical area to determine what items will both represent their location and fit in a box that is 18 by 24 by 8 inches. Some classes selected a plastic bag filled with sand to represent the beaches on Long Island and a picture of Teddy Roosevelt, who had a home in the area. Classes in other states complete similar research and select items for their artifact box. When a partner class's unidentified box arrives, students begin to unravel the clues to determine the location of the partner class. This long-term project, which links to the classroom curriculum, draws on a variety of reference materials and requires students to analyze and classify data. Best of all, by design, it actively involves each student. The Artifact Box unit provides all students with the opportunity to learn the process skills of research, critical thinking, problem solving, and decision making. This type of activity also teaches the skills needed for more in-depth small-group and individual enrichment to pursue a Type III activity.

The strength of the STELLAR program lies in the unique ways it is put into practice in different schools in the district. In 2005, Joan Waldman, the principal of Watson Elementary School, along with STELLAR teacher Trish Montemarano and academic support teacher Susan Kahan, designed "Pursuing Passions," a Type III schoolwide enrichment project. Students selected an area of interest, acquired a deeper level of knowledge on the topic and used public speaking skills to share their passion. As students participated in the Passions Fair, they were introduced to others' interests and passions—a Type I experience. (See Figure 3.1 for more information about the project.)

A High School Model: English 9A

In the spring of 2004, we met with our 9th grade English teachers to initiate the design of the pre-IB curriculum for English 9. Although the classes had been detracked previously, we felt that the curriculum needed additional leveling-up. The data that we compiled after successfully implementing such a course of study for all 10th grade students in English and social studies in 2003 framed our initial discussion. Teachers expressed concerns regarding the maturity and independence of 9th graders transitioning from middle school to high school. Would they be able to devote their attention to a more challenging course, given the anxiety students feel during such a transition?

The teachers set out to address their own concerns by developing guidelines for the course. Student responsibilities would need to be clearly delineated to both the students and the parents. All assignments would have specific deadlines, and any long-term project would include interim due dates. Assessment rubrics would be reviewed with students at the start of every assignment. Instructional strategies would be devised to meet the needs of learners at all achievement levels. Teachers decided to incorporate graphic organizers, student choice, literature circles, text-based seminars, jigsaw techniques, read-alouds, and reflections into the course. The seeds of the new curriculum were planted.

FIGURE 3.1

Pursuing Passions:
An Individualized Elementary Enrichment Project

Imagine every student in an entire school researching topics about which they are passionate. Imagine giving students the time and opportunity to discover where their passions lie. Then imagine being able to help them explain and share their interest with others. That is just what took place during the 2005–2006 school year at Watson Elementary School.

Prior to the 2005 summer vacation, a schoolwide assembly was held to introduce the Pursuing Passions project. The meaning of the word *passion* was explained, and students were encouraged to search for a passion of their own. A letter was sent home to parents so that they could help their child recognize and identify potential passions. In early September, the forms were collected and the information was collated so that material at the appropriate reading level could be ordered—an essential component to ensuring the successful outcome of the endeavor.

In the fall, a Teachers' Passion Fair was held in the gym to demonstrate the types of passions teachers had and to model how to give topic presentations using essential questions. Music from the 1950s, performed by one of the 5th grade teachers, had everyone rockin' and rollin'. One teacher shared her passion for crocheting, and this presentation spearheaded the formation of a 5th grade crochet club, which now makes blankets and donates them to local hospitals.

Intermediate students at Watson then chose a topic and embarked on a yearlong investigative journey. Through individual conferences, students were encouraged to develop higher-level questions about their passion. They read, took notes, and read some more. Students learned to paraphrase as they wrote introductions, pay attention to the use of voice in writing, revise, edit, and put their presentations together in a variety of ways. The project culminated with the Students' Passions Fair, where students used their public speaking skills to teach others about what they had learned.

Needless to say, the process took a long time from start to finish, but the finished products were well worth the effort. The range of student passions was astounding. From lighthouses to architecture, from the care of dogs to the care of snakes, from fashion to Shakespeare, students practiced the skills needed for acquiring and disseminating in-depth knowledge, and they had fun doing it!

Source: Joan Waldman, Susan Kahan, and Trish Montemarano, Floyd B. Watson Elementary School, Rockville Centre, New York. Used with permission.

The team began the project, using the backwards planning model. During the first full day of planning, teachers engaged in thoughtful, professional conversation as a recorder documented their thinking in the planner. Notes that emerged from the process included the following:

- *Core beliefs:* We can meet the needs of all students as we raise the level of instruction.
- *Mandates:* Prepare all students for English IB 11.
- *Understandings:* All people, regardless of time period, race, religion, or sex come to a divide between innocence and experience. Crossing this divide involves a complexity of thoughts and emotions.
- *Essential questions:* How can we apply literature to life?
- *Knowledge:* The form and function of literary elements.
- *Skills:* Finding commonalities between two works of literature.
- *Assessment:* Process rubric = 50 percent of grade; product rubric = 50 percent of grade.
- *Instructional strategies:* Teach for depth. Less is more.
- *Timeline:* Short story unit at beginning that introduces students to literary devices.
- *Resources:* Include tapes of all books and short stories in the curriculum.

The team shared the notes from the initial meeting with the entire English department, soliciting feedback, suggestions, and comments. At a follow-up professional development curriculum planning session that included the 9th grade teachers and the assistant superintendent for curriculum, the team finalized literature selections, created mandated assessments, determined the structure of student portfolios, outlined a research project, and finalized grading rubrics.

Three teachers from the planning team agreed to synthesize the discussion documents into a formal curriculum. The curriculum followed the district's template, including an introduction, goals, course outline, assessment plans, bibliography, and learning standards. The course outline identified each unit of study, with a time allotment and specific objectives.

The outline also addressed the related learning standard, instructional resources, applicable reading and writing strategies, and the level of Bloom's taxonomy for each objective.

Such features are critical to the development of curricula that will be taught to a heterogeneous group of learners. For example, the inclusion of reading and writing strategies helps teachers meet the needs of struggling learners while promoting reading and writing across the curriculum. Identifying Bloom's taxonomy levels ensures that higher-level thinking skills and deeper understandings are promoted for all students, especially high achievers. The last two components focus the curriculum writers on the district's priorities of literacy across each curriculum area and teaching for deeper understanding.

An additional feature of the curriculum that was developed with heterogeneity in mind was teacher-created product and process rubrics for student assessment. The process rubric for English, which can be found in Appendix A of this book, was developed to help all students, especially lower achievers, be successful in the new curriculum, separately from their accomplishments with regard to classroom products. After some lively debate, the teachers agreed that 50 percent of a student's grade would be derived from the teacher's assessment of student progress using the process rubric.

In mid-July, the curriculum writing team shared a draft of the curriculum with the assistant superintendent for curriculum and the building principal. The entire 9th grade team reconvened in August to review the curriculum, offer suggestions, and finalize the portfolio process. The final curriculum document is the canon for each teacher of the 9A English course. It is not a suggested curriculum, but rather a *mandated* curriculum. Each teacher adheres to the timeline of instruction, teaches the designated literature selections at the same time, and evaluates students using the specified assessments.

A K–8 Model for Mathematics

In *Principles and Standards for School Mathematics,* the National Council for Teachers of Mathematics (2000) defines its equity principle in mathematics: "Excellence in mathematics education requires equity—high expectations and strong support for all students" (p. 1). Our district's mathematics curriculum now reflects this principle. We offer all students a high-quality, rigorous program of instruction in heterogeneous classes and provide support for struggling students. This third example provides insight into how we created a successful detracked, accelerated program in mathematics.

As described in Chapter 1, even after we "opened the gates" to the middle school accelerated math program, we were appalled to realize that racial and socioeconomic stratification of students still existed in the two tracks. The regular class had taken on the characteristics of the former "skills" class: minority and special education students were overrepresented, academic achievement was low, and students were disruptive (Burris, 2003). Students in the new lower-track class experienced what Oakes and Lipton (2003) call the self-fulfilling prophecy of low expectations, coupled with fewer opportunities and poor academic performance. We concluded that providing choice was not the way to help all students achieve excellence in mathematics (see Yonezawa et al., 2002).

The New York State Education Department mandates that all middle schools offer students the opportunity to accelerate in mathematics in grade 8, that is, to complete the 9th grade curriculum (then called Sequential I Mathematics) by the end of grade 8. As the middle school detracked, accelerated mathematics for all students became the only option for providing a single rigorous course of study in a heterogeneous class setting. This change was not an easy sell to teachers, despite the fact that data and research supported the decision. For example, even though nearly half of all 8th graders were in the accelerated course, the median score was consistently 95 percent. Also, the Third International Mathematics and Science Study had found that 8th graders successfully complete algebra courses in countries around the world. We asked, "Why not teach algebra to all students in Rockville Centre?"

We implemented our K–8 mathematics curriculum in two phases, the first based on the New York state Sequential I Mathematics curriculum and Regents exam (in 1995) and the second on the New York State Mathematics

A curriculum and Regents exam (in 2002).* Sequential I Mathematics, a one-year course, included all algebra typically taught in a first-year high school course, with the integration of statistics, probability, logic, and some geometry. The Mathematics A course, proposed as a one-and-a-half-year curriculum, included all of the Sequential I topics and added a full semester of high school geometry content.

During the 1994–1995 school year, we formed a math curriculum committee composed of 10 elementary teachers (a 4th and a 5th grade teacher from each of the five elementary buildings); 9 middle school math teachers, equally representing each grade from 6 to 8; and coauthor Delia Garrity, who was then the middle school assistant principal and supervisor of the math department. The elementary school teachers were included because Superintendent William H. Johnson, after consulting the principal and assistant principal at the middle school, decided that the math curriculum in grades 4–6 would change concurrently with the upper-level courses in order to support the acceleration of the curriculum.

We used the backwards planning model, beginning with an analysis of the requirements of the Sequential I Mathematics Regents course. A team of teachers and administrators then examined the New York State standards and core curriculum for grades 4–8, comparing those documents with the present curriculum in grades 4–8. They found that even though all five elementary schools nominally taught the same curriculum in grades 4 and 5, there were inconsistencies among the schools: Some teachers followed the outline via a textbook, while others only loosely adhered to the prescribed curriculum and in many cases did not teach all required topics. This inconsistency had to be eliminated to establish a firm, consistent foundation for instruction at the middle school level.

The committee compacted five years of curriculum into four by taking the following steps:

*The New York State Education Department phased out the Sequential Mathematics high school program and replaced it with two courses called Mathematics A and Mathematics B. These courses are now being replaced by Integrated Algebra, Integrated Geometry, and Integrated Trigonometry.

1. They eliminated the reintroduction of topics each year and replaced that strategy with spiraling reinforcement and application activities.

2. They designed the curriculum so that each topic was taught in depth, rather than introducing a concept and applying it on only a superficial level.

3. They moved the introduction of a few concepts to a lower grade level.

For example, the 5th grade curriculum originally included teaching both the skills and applications of adding and subtracting fractions. The 6th grade curriculum reintroduced these skills and continued with multiplying and dividing fractions. In the new curriculum, all fraction skills and applications are taught in grade 5. In grade 6, students review these skills when they learn how to solve equations containing fractions.

At the same time that the district began using the accelerated math curriculum for all students, the Board of Education funded three additional teaching periods so there could be math support classes in grades 6–8. This funding allows a struggling math student to attend a heterogeneously grouped accelerated math class every day and then receive help every other day, in a support class taught by a math teacher. The curriculum for the math support class focuses on pre-teaching, reteaching, and reinforcing concepts that are being taught in the accelerated math class. For example, if the teacher plans to introduce solving equations with integers, the teacher of the support class will review operations with integers and pre-teach the basic application in an equation.

The second phase of revising the math curriculum, enrolling all 8th grade students in Math A, required a more dramatic change in program. Math A is typically completed at the end of the first semester of 10th grade. For the first three years of implementation of Math A, all students in Rockville Centre took the Math A Regents exam in January of 9th grade. After the first year, the high school math teachers believed that it was not in the students' best interest to complete the Math A curriculum and prepare for the Regents exam during their first semester in high school. The teachers requested that we further accelerate the students and complete the entire

Math A curriculum and the Regents exam by the end of 8th grade. The middle school math teachers analyzed the curricula for grades 6–8 and suggested that we begin implementing this change with the incoming 6th grade class.

In order to accommodate the extra semester of instruction by the end of grade 8, we decided to replace the 5th grade curriculum with a 6th grade level mathematics program that uses a constructivist approach to emphasize deep mathematical thinking, problem solving, and communication. At the same time, we introduced a similar mathematics program in grades K–4. Elementary school teachers, particularly 5th grade teachers, were somewhat overwhelmed by the change. Extensive professional development focusing on math content and instructional strategies proved to be the vital component in the successful implementation of the present-day K–8 curriculum. Chapter 5 provides a more detailed description of the professional development model used to support the change in the elementary curriculum.

Supervisors' Role in the Curriculum Process

Instructional leadership is critical to the success of any education reform. Revising the curriculum is essential to effective detracking, and the process requires the active participation and encouragement of school leaders. During each step of curriculum design in our district, the assistant superintendent for curriculum and instruction or the curriculum coordinator for grades K–12 is part of the process. A member of the curriculum staff— and when possible, a building administrator—participates in professional meetings with teachers to review the current curriculum and assessment data. The team identifies patterns within the data, both globally and specifically. Comparisons of students' performance in each track or level of study typically expose a disparity in both the curriculum and instruction. Using the data, curriculum leaders provide teachers with a clear explanation of the rationale and goals of a new curriculum.

When the curriculum revision is complete, the assistant superintendent for curriculum and instruction reads and evaluates each curriculum document to ensure that the final product meets the district's standards of a rigorous, high-level course of study for heterogeneously grouped classes, thus preventing the "watering down" of curriculum. But the process does not end there. The building administrators and central office curriculum administrators carefully monitor curriculum implementation. The articulation of the course among the teachers, and with their supervisors, must be consistent. Building administrators read weekly lesson plans, informally and formally observe all staff members, and attend grade-level or department meetings. The curriculum staff meets with teachers of a new secondary curriculum at least once a semester to monitor the established timeline for instruction, assess the effectiveness of the instructional materials, and review samples of student work. The review of student work is a powerful tool for assessing both student understanding and teacher adherence to the new curriculum.

At the elementary level, teachers participate in monthly sessions to ensure a consistent, unified program of instruction across the five elementary buildings. The structure for these sessions is detailed in the section on professional development in Chapter 5.

As you begin to develop curriculum for detracked classes, consider the following questions:

1. Does the present curriculum development process allow for sufficient teacher input?

2. What can be done to ensure that all who teach the course have a voice in its development?

3. What can be done to make sure that all learners can be successful and challenged by the curriculum?

4. What support services and materials can be provided for students who struggle?

5. What can be done to ensure that the curriculum will be implemented and taught as intended?

Involving Teachers in Curriculum Creation

When encouraged to take part in curriculum design, teachers feel liberated, rather than restricted by externally imposed mandates. Our STELLAR teachers received training in the enrichment model, designed the instructional process, and continue to create units of study based on their collaboration with classroom teachers. They still meet monthly to share instructional materials, research units of common interest, and participate in training on the use of technology. Our 9th grade English teachers made decisions about the content of their course and designed the assessment rubrics to be used. Teachers evaluated literature based on the components of the curriculum planner, determined the literature selections, and selected additional literary pieces as extension activities. Our mathematics teachers devised methods to compact the curriculum, designated the timeline for instruction, and selected instructional materials. Teachers share specific lesson plans and divide the workload as they teach the same topics at the same time. Teachers have ownership of the course and the curriculum, and all students receive the same high-quality, rigorous curriculum.

When a curriculum is initially designed, written, and implemented, the teachers of the course meet regularly, as part of their professional development, to ensure adherence to the curriculum and to tweak components. In some cases, teachers will enhance the curriculum to meet the instructional needs of the students in their heterogeneous classes by adding resources, strategies, and common projects. The goals, objectives, and standards remain intact, but the delivery of instruction or assessment tools may change. A responsive, dynamic curriculum allows teachers to address district goals in an organized, coherent manner.

Concluding Thoughts on Curriculum Development

For us, detracked classes are nonnegotiable. When school leaders and the Board of Education decided to group students heterogeneously, we did so based on experience, data, and, most of all, our belief about the democratic purposes of the public school. The development process and the content are negotiable, and within the control of the curriculum development team. What has been most interesting for us to observe is how often the impetus to detrack a course now comes from our teachers. They have seen the benefits of detracking, and they trust that they are welcome members of the team that creates the curriculum.

As we created a culture in which teachers believe that students learn best in detracked classes, it was equally important to achieve the same culture with parents. When educators visit our district we are always asked, "How do you convince parents that their children will not suffer academically if struggling students are included in their classes?" This is, of course, a pivotal question that guides the politics involved in making the change. Chapter 4 will examine the strategies that we employed, and continue to employ, as we engage in the delicate politics of detracking.

The Politics
of Detracking

It would seem that detracking *should* be easy. It is a matter of deciding to reorganize the way that students are assigned to classes, then phasing in the changes over time. As tracks are eliminated, the school puts in place a curriculum designed to give all students access to excellence. However, anyone who has engaged in detracking in even a limited way has quickly learned that detracking is a difficult and potentially treacherous reform to implement (Wells & Oakes, 1996). It takes hard work, courage, vigilance, and a willingness to challenge commonly held assumptions about students' capacity to learn. When such assumptions are challenged in schools, political battles follow. As Oakes, Quartz, Ryan, and Lipton (2000) wisely observe in *Becoming Good American Schools,* "If reform were to be welcome and consistent with the existing culture, it would not be reform at all; it would simply be a slightly altered status quo" (p. 24).

The political battles that often accompany detracking can be both daunting and exhausting. The purpose of this chapter is not to dissuade schools from embarking on this important reform, but to prepare them. If school leaders understand why detracking quickly becomes a political battle, they can more effectively respond to the resistance that will develop as they introduce the reform.

But understanding the "why" of resistance is not enough; ways must be found to counter that resistance. We will share what we and others have done to successfully neutralize resistance—sometimes winning over non-believers, or when that is not possible, presenting effective counterarguments to allow detracking to move forward. It has been our experience that once detracking gets traction, the benefits of the reform become evident, and the reform takes hold.

What We Know from Research

Much has been written about detracking reforms that have struggled or have been derailed by political resistance. Oakes and colleagues (Oakes, Wells, Jones, & Datnow, 1997; Oakes et al., 2000), Wells and Serena (1996), and Welner (2001) have studied such reforms and written extensively on the topic. These researchers offer insights on how detracking reforms might falter, and we highly recommend that you read their studies, which recount the political forces that surprised well-meaning school leaders who sought to implement detracking.

Public schools are political spaces, and therefore the same forces that drive national politics influence the agenda of school reform. Think for a moment about why Americans gravitate toward political parties. Generally, citizens align themselves with candidates or parties that they believe best represent their beliefs and self-interests. Beliefs about the role of religion in public life or the morality of the death penalty or abortion influence how votes are cast. Likewise, voters often consider self-interest when choosing whether to support tax policies or social security regulations.

The same two forces operate when schools propose detracking. Beliefs about intelligence and equity evoke emotional responses from parents and teachers. In addition, the self-interests of those who believe that their children are well-served by tracking are threatened by the idea of detracking, and that threat moves them to political action.

Researchers have carefully identified the beliefs and self-interests that sustain tracking (see Oakes, 2005; Wells & Serena, 1996). They have also documented what occurs when schools attempt to detrack—those who oppose the reform quickly perceive a threat to their interests, and they attempt to get out in front of the reform and stop it. Political alliances are formed, and the local school board is besieged by the opposition.

The most common alliances opposing detracking form between the teachers of high-track classes, who enjoy teaching the school's most motivated students, and the parents of high-track students. Parents of students identified as gifted often exercise political clout and attempt to block the reform. The risk of "bright flight" (and, in integrated districts, "white flight") often leads supporters of detracking to back off or offer modifications to appease special interest groups (Oakes, 2005).

Our experience has taught us, however, that if educators are willing to weather the storm and stand up to resistance as soon as it begins, detracking can move forward. As its benefits become apparent, resistance will wane. In the following section, we summarize our experiences with political resistance by focusing on what we call the Three Ps that sustain tracking—prejudice, prestige, and power. We will discuss each of these three forces and present strategies to help school communities work through the obstacles that the Three Ps present.

Prejudice

The practice of tracking is based on the belief that the capacity to learn is shaped by biology and childhood environment, and that there is little that schools can do to affect learning capacity, commonly referred to as *ability*. This logic suggests that if we were to correctly determine ability, group students of like ability together, and then tailor curriculum accordingly, teaching and learning would be more effective. Many educators, policy-makers, and parents subscribe to this reasoning, despite considerable evidence that tracking is harmful to many students (Oakes, 2005) and that tracked classes are rarely homogeneous in makeup (Useem, 1992a, 1992b; Welner, 2001). They believe that teachers cannot effectively address the needs of students who differ in achievement in one classroom.

Prejudice and the Construction of Ability

The idea that in order for students to learn they must be grouped with students of similar ability is based on two misconceptions. The first is that the way we label students is scientific and measurable rather than, as some scholars have suggested, subjective and prejudiced (Oakes & Lipton, 1999). The second is that heterogeneity hinders learning, because teachers must "teach to the middle," forgoing the needs of struggling students and high achievers. The combination of these misconceptions led schools to sort students into different groups for instruction.

The labeling and sorting of students began at the beginning of the 20th century, when schools became more inclusive. For the first time, schools were asked to educate the children of immigrants and the sons and daughters of working-class families, instead of focusing solely on the middle class and upper echelons of society. Tracking was seen as the way to both accommodate the needs of these new students, who were deemed to have lesser ability, and preserve the role of schools as preparation for college-bound students (Oakes & Lipton, 1999).

Although our society has moved beyond the rigid stereotypes of the past, many of us still view the school's role as the "sorter and selector" of students' futures. Parents who hold high academic ambitions for their students often express the fear that if students with lower achievement are in the child's class, opportunities will be lost to their child. In short, it is assumed that students who learn differently, or who do not grasp material quickly, will disrupt the learning of higher-achieving students.

A few years ago, a group of teachers and administrators from a high school similar to Rockville Centre came for a visit. These visitors were interested in learning more about our IB classes, which we encourage all students to take. During part of the day, the visiting teachers met with teachers and building leaders. The Advanced Placement history teacher from the visiting school opined that only top students should be in her class. Her reasoning was that lower-achieving students simply had "nothing to offer the class." A shocked silence fell upon the room as our teachers, and her colleagues, reflected on what they had heard.

The teacher's remark epitomizes the intellectual prejudice that is prevalent in many highly tracked schools. To believe that a student who does not read or write as well as another, or who comes from a less privileged home with fewer academic resources, cannot provide rich insights during class discussions is a prejudice. Often, it is the question of the less confident student that sparks the alternate explanation that helps all students achieve a deeper understanding. We do not believe that students exist to further the goals of the classes, but that classes exist for the sake of students. Whether to allow a student access to the best curriculum should not depend upon what he or she has "to offer."

Because so many of us were educated in tracked schools, we are comfortable with our intellectual prejudices, and we do not question whether tracking is fair or effective. Many assume that the curriculum in detracked classes will be watered down as teachers teach to the middle. They argue that students with weaker skills will be frustrated and act out. This might be true if no accommodations are made for struggling learners. The traditional talk-and-chalk model, paced to the learning speed of the average student, is not effective in detracked classes. However, frustration can be avoided by introducing student-centered teaching strategies. New research on constructivism and differentiated instruction, which we will discuss in Chapter 6, demonstrates that the needs of all learners can be met in heterogeneous classes with planning and forethought.

Concerns based on intellectual prejudices and misconceptions about what constitutes good instruction should not be dismissed out of hand, however. Schools must take considerable care to ensure that classes are both rigorous and fair, and that all students are involved in, and challenged by, the curriculum. As discussed in the previous chapter, schools must carefully ensure that the former high-track, enriched curriculum is incorporated into the curriculum of the detracked class. It is the job of educational leaders to reassure parents that teachers will teach a rich curriculum and not teach to the middle, whatever that might mean to them.

It is also the job of educational leaders to ensure that high-quality instruction is given to all students.

The strategy of teaching the high-track curriculum in detracked classes is not unique to our district; it is the strategy proposed by scholars who support detracking (Slavin & Braddock, 1993; Wheelock, 1992). Parents of struggling students should understand that to prevent frustration, scaffolding and differentiated strategies will be used, and support systems will be provided.

Thinking through ways to respond to concerns of parents and teachers is vital. You cannot simply dismiss them. Instead, you must acknowledge that teaching strategies will change and be prepared to provide examples of how those strategies will be implemented in the classroom.

Some parents will still continue to argue against heterogeneous classes because they want to isolate their children from other students who, they believe, are not as bright. These parents want something special, and curriculum is not their concern at all. At an elementary school PTA meeting, a parent questioned the superintendent as to why there was not an isolated program for gifted students. The school provides an enrichment program, but all students get it, which she said was not enough. In response, Superintendent Johnson asked a simple question of the PTA: "Who in this room does not have a child who has gifts and talents?" Not one parent raised their hand. Sincere efforts to help parents understand the philosophy of excellence with equity can be highly effective.

Racial and Class Prejudice

The prejudice that supports tracking goes beyond faulty assumptions about learning capacity, however. As mentioned in the previous chapter, our district is ethnically and socioeconomically diverse; that diversity makes detracking a more rewarding and, at the same time, a more complicated process. We were rewarded by seeing achievement gaps narrow as we detracked; our success was complicated by the racial prejudice and fear that occasionally bubbled to the surface. Our experience is not unique. Detracking reforms are the most difficult to accomplish in racially integrated schools in which tracking has resulted in de facto segregation in classes (George, 1992; Wells & Serena, 1996). At times, such prejudice is blatant; at other times, it is masked.

One of the authors first encountered the connection between tracking and racial prejudice during a parent conference in the early 1990s. At the time, she was a teacher in a tracked, integrated middle school on Long Island. During the conference, the student's father told her that he wanted his daughter in the honors class the following year so that "she would not be in class with the black kids." While other statements we have encountered may not be as blatantly discriminatory, they often reflect carefully coded racial and class prejudices: "I thought this was the year you were going to weed *those* kids out." Whether such statements are blunt or couched in more politically correct language, the message is the same.

After studying the detracking process in 10 integrated schools, Oakes, Wells, Jones, and Datnow (1997) concluded that much of this resistance is based on long-standing incorrect assumptions regarding race and intelligence. Some of the conclusions that are drawn come, in a self-perpetuating manner, from the negative results of tracking itself. In tracked schools, African American and Latino students are less likely to be placed in high-track classes than are their white or Asian counterparts with the same achievement test scores (Vanfossen et al., 1987), and they are overrepresented in low-track classes, further reinforcing false stereotypes (Heubert & Hauser, 1999).

Even in districts that pride themselves on equitable and forward-thinking policies, stratification often exists. We were surprised to find that prior to detracking mathematics in our middle school, nearly half of all high-achieving minority students (students with nationally standardized math stanine scores of 8 or 9) had not taken the high-track, accelerated mathematics course. However, nearly 100 percent of high-achieving white and Asian students had done so. When tracking was eliminated and all students were taking accelerated mathematics, not only were all high-achieving minority students successful in the accelerated mathematics program, they also all completed a course in either pre-calculus or Advanced Placement calculus prior to high school graduation (Burris et al., 2006).

It is important to note that even if schools are not racially integrated, other types of stratification can occur. In nearly every district, social class prejudices work to keep students apart. A highly proficient student from a low socioeconomic background has only slightly better than a 50 percent chance of being placed in a high-track class (Vanfossen et al., 1987). Professional parents, who understand the benefits of high-track classes, are highly successful at "working the system" to ensure that their children are placed in the top-track classes (Useem, 1992a). Because of their own post–high school educational experiences, they understand the importance of their child taking the most rigorous curriculum that a school has to offer. Thus, tracked schools become stratified not only by race but also by social class.

Disaggregating achievement data can demonstrate why detracking is needed in diverse schools with achievement gaps. You can't close the achievement gap until you close the curriculum gap. Our superintendent skillfully uses the mandate of No Child Left Behind to convince the community of the importance of all children having access to the best curriculum. "Closing the gap" data are presented at board meetings and PTA meetings. We have been able to clearly demonstrate a positive relationship between detracking and the number of minority students, students who receive free or reduced-priced lunch, and special education students who achieve a Regents diploma (Burris & Welner, 2005; Burris, Wiley, Welner, & Murphy, 2008).

When prejudice rears its ugly head, respond in a polite but firm way. State that your school is committed to ensuring that all students receive the best education that the school can offer. Talk about gaps rather than hiding them. Do not be held hostage by threats of "flight." The increases in overall achievement that accompany detracking will attract families who care about education to your district. Remember that the school scores shown to prospective homebuyers encompass the scores of all students, not just students in the high-track classes.

Prestige

Recently we interviewed an experienced science teacher for a high school position. When he was asked why he wished to leave his school, he replied, "Right now I am teaching AP, but a teacher is coming back from maternity leave and they are going to be leveling me down." For this teacher, teaching kids who were not the "top" kids was a perceived as a demotion.

Teacher Prestige

It's common for teachers to perceive their prestige as linked to the course they teach. According to Oakes and Lipton (1999), teachers of high-track classes have higher status in the eyes of colleagues and families than do teachers of low-track classes. Oakes and Lipton note that while teachers of low-achieving students receive sympathy for how difficult their job can be, it is assumed that they do not have the depth of content knowledge that high-track teachers have. Sadly, there is some basis in fact for these assumptions. High-track math and science classes are more likely to be taught by teachers who are both better qualified and more experienced (Oakes, Ormseth, Bell, & Camp, 1990); less qualified or less experienced teachers more often teach low-track classes. Finley (1984) found that the skills of teachers assigned to low-track classes appear to diminish over time, providing low-track students with lesser-quality instruction.

As we began to implement heterogeneous classes, the greatest resistance came from veteran teachers who were accustomed to teaching the high-track classes. Their assignments were prestigious, and their pedagogy and lesson plans had proven successful for teaching highly motivated students. If the students did not succeed, it was deemed to be the student's fault, and they were moved to lower-track classes.

Students in lower-track classes believed that they did not get the school's best teachers, and in some cases, they were correct. Some schools consider the teaching of high-track classes a perk reserved for talented veteran teachers, and they assign problem teachers to low-track classes as punishment.

Over time, we began to adopt the philosophy that teachers should not own courses, and that every teacher's typical schedule would include both an IB course and a Regents-level course. This made the transition to heterogeneous grouping easier. When principals create an elite faculty who believe that they are entitled to teach the high achievers only, you can expect that some will oppose any initiatives increasing heterogeneity in their classes. Dispersing a teacher's assignments across tracks sends the signal that all students' education is important. This, however, is an interim solution. Heterogeneous grouping provides the best solution of all. When detracked classes become the norm, all students have an equal opportunity to study with the most qualified teachers. We also found that teachers who struggled when teaching low-track classes feel better about their teaching when high achievers are in the class, and their skills begin to improve.

Parent Prestige

Parents feel pride when their children are selected for gifted programs or honors classes. Schools often speak about their "gifted parents" as though the parents, not the students, have academic talent. When detracking begins, and all students have access to the best curriculum, the parents of students who are high achievers may feel a loss of prestige.

It is both wise and fair to ensure that high-achieving students can still develop their talents and have them recognized. Although our schools are detracked, we continue to provide a wonderful science research program in which all students may participate if they choose. This program allows talented students to pursue their interests in depth and participate in prestigious competitions. In addition, we have many academic competitions in which students can participate. Teachers regularly provide information regarding special summer programs that challenge students, and counselors nominate students for prestigious academic awards. In the 10th grade, students may take an elective class in advanced math topics in addition to their regular math class. We understand the importance of pride in academic achievement. We just don't let prestige hijack our school system.

Power

Whenever there is a challenge to the status quo, those who have benefited in the past are bound to be unhappy. During their longitudinal study of 10 racially integrated schools that were undergoing a detracking reform, Wells and Oakes (1996) observed that

> Powerful parents of the students who have succeeded and even excelled in the current system are often able to maintain the status quo, despite educational research that suggests that a new system could better serve all students. These powerful parents demand something in return for their commitment to public education—for keeping their children in public schools, as opposed to fleeing to the private schools that many could afford. (p. 139)

Indeed the threat of bright flight is often intimidating enough to halt many school reforms that would benefit the majority of students. As we mentioned earlier, it's when such parents align themselves with the teachers of high-track classes who also have an interest in preserving the status quo that many tracking reforms come to a halt.

In addition, in tracked systems where teacher recommendations and grades decide track placement, a considerable amount of power is given to teachers. Disruptive students are often moved to lower tracks. Because recommendations and grades vary from teacher to teacher, not all students have equitable access to honors, IB, and AP programs. A poor class-participation grade can affect a student's chance of getting into a high-track class. Teachers, counselors, and administrators are often afraid of not giving the children of powerful parents the recommendation needed for high-track placement. In short, power issues related to track placement are messy. Nevertheless, while most educators breathe a sigh of relief when they disappear with detracking, a few are loath to let them go.

Advice for Confronting the Three *P*s

To pretend that the Three *P*s do not exist is foolhardy. Still, honest discussions about prejudice, prestige, and power make educators and parents uncomfortable, and are thus hard to begin. We suggest that as an introduction to these conversations, you begin by collecting and discussing the following data with your school's or district's stakeholders:

• *Demographic data.* Collect and analyze the proportions of student groups in each class level or track by race, geographic area of town, and socioeconomic status. Do patterns emerge? What do these data tell us about equity and tracking?

 • *Resource data.* Collect and analyze data about the outside resources available to students. Which students have access to tutors, music lessons, summer programs, and prep courses for SATs? Is there a connection between resources and the data collected above? If so, what do such data tell us about tracking as a meritocracy?

 • *Teacher data.* Collect and analyze data about the years of experience and educational credentials of teachers by course and track level. Do any patterns emerge? Analyze the teaching assignments by teacher for a five-year period. How often do assignments vary? Do teachers teach across grade levels and tracks, or are teachers "tracked" themselves?

When schools mull over the data, people begin to discuss how the Three *P*s affect students' and teachers' lives. Carefully guided discussions can help schools overcome resistance by facilitating others' understanding of the complicated social processes that sustain tracking.

Listening to Resistance

Prior to detracking, our school district put tremendous resources into low-track classes, to little or no avail, and these disappointing results were not unique. The National Research Council concluded that students should not be educated in low-track classes due to the overwhelming amount of research that found negative effects stemming from low-track classes (Heubert & Hauser, 1999). Few parents who argue for the continuation of low-track classes would want their children in them.

Still, no matter how carefully you share data or follow the process we have outlined so far, there will be those who resist. They will insist that the current tracked system can be fixed rather than altered. They will tell you to spread talented teachers around (as long as their child still winds up in a talented teacher's class). They will say that the better answer for students who are doing poorly is additional remedial services, even as you present data documenting the ineffectiveness of remediation and low-track classes. They will tell you to give the same curriculum to all children, just at different times and in different classes. Any statements that contain racial or class biases will be coded, but everyone in the room will know what is being said and what is feared.

During one meeting prior to implementing heterogeneous classes in the 10th grade, a parent asked, "Why do we need to get rid of the tracks to challenge all students? Why don't you just raise the ceiling on the high-track class and the ceiling on the low-track class as well?" One of our teachers wisely replied, "We are not talking about raising the ceiling of learning; we want to rip the ceiling off for every student." That should be the intent of detracking—creating classrooms where each child is given the opportunity to excel. It is important to communicate that goal to parents, illustrate it with examples of how you plan to achieve it, and maintain the bottom line: that tracking cannot be reformed, although many have tried.

With the emergence of e-mail and cell phones, it is very easy for alliances to organize quickly, and it is not unusual to be blindsided at a public meeting. Our best advice is to be prepared with facts, listen politely to concerns, address issues as best you can, and stand your ground. Once we enacted pre-IB courses for all 10th graders, parents—even those who were early critics—gave the practice high praise. It is also helpful to have supportive teachers attend meetings where detracking might be discussed. We have observed that when parents understand that detracking is supported by teachers as well as by administrators, opposition decreases.

Detracking with Community Involvement

Although we do not have experience using grass roots community organizations or the courts to help detrack schools, additional strategies may be needed in large school systems, especially where tracking has been used to promote in-school segregation, or when there appears to be no motivation to promote equity from within the system. Kevin Welner and Jeannie Oakes have documented such reform efforts, and their research provides sound advice and guidance (Welner, 2001; Welner & Oakes, 2000). When detracking reform meets with resistance, they suggest the following strategies:

1. *Commit to the principles of the detracking reform.* Explain equity issues to the public and to staff. Challenge the assumptions that support low expectations. As the reform plan is developed, establish long-term goals that are commensurate with the belief that all students can learn and that all deserve access to a school's best instruction.

2. *Engage all of the community in the discussion.* Make sure that all voices are heard, especially those voices that are generally underrepresented in the district's political discussions. Focus all discussions on equity and excellence. Make sure that faculty/parent study groups include members from all parts of the community and all demographic groups.

3. *Provide incentives to teachers who are willing to take on the challenge of teaching heterogeneous classes.* Faculty study groups can produce teachers who are willing to take a leadership role in the reform. They will approach the challenge with commitment and enthusiasm. As resistant teachers retire, replace them with reform-minded faculty.

4. *Phase out all low-track classes.* Establish minimal, college preparatory benchmarks for all students. Provide the academic support and counseling that students need to be successful.

Responding to Fear and Anxiety

The greatest fear of parents of former high-track students is that detracking reform will compromise their child's education. They understand how students who were not in the top track will benefit, but they worry that such a benefit will come at their child's expense.

That is where good leadership comes in. It is not enough to say that the high-track curriculum will be taught to all students; school leaders must be intimately involved in the curriculum development process. From beginning to end, our district's assistant superintendent was involved in the development of the heterogeneous 10th grade English and social studies curriculum. We needed to make sure that what we promised parents was true, so teachers went about creating the best course of studies that they could. The curriculum was challenging yet accessible, with all assessments preparing students not only for the New York State Regents exams, but for the IB courses in 11th grade. Although we developed techniques for differentiating the delivery of instruction, we never differentiated goals for learning.

We did, however, assess student learning in more sophisticated ways. We created both process and product rubrics to evaluate student work. Portfolio assessments and projects were integrated into the course. An every-other-day support class for struggling students was transformed from a remedial model to a class that supported the curriculum through pre-reading, scaffolding, and analysis. The district bought inexpensive paperbacks so that students could annotate and highlight them, just as they would in college.

Several years later, a small group of parents expressed concern that their children were not getting enough work or challenge in the heterogeneous class. In response to the concern, teachers created extension activities for each marking period to create challenge and foster independent learning. Interestingly enough, few children chose to do the extension activities, and they were not all high achievers. However, they were students who really wanted to enrich their learning, and they took advantage of the opportunity to learn more about what the class was studying.

Some parents of students who struggle will worry that an enriched curriculum will put undue stress on their child, or that their child will not be academically successful. Good supports are essential to countering this concern. Generous extra help should be available. A clear process rubric will help students understand what they need to do to be successful in the class. Of greatest importance, teachers need to reflect on practices and be supported in developing new strategies and methodology. Our district's extensive program of differentiated instruction will be described in Chapters 5 and 6.

Finally, faculty will worry that they will have difficulty meeting the needs of all learners. In a tracked system, where unsuccessful students can be moved down the ranks, the burden of learning is primarily on the student. When all students are included in the classroom, the primary burden shifts to the teacher. Teachers will worry that they will feel pressure to slow down the curriculum or that parents will complain if some students earn low grades. Encouragement and support from administrators and supervisors are essential. The work that teachers do should be recognized and appreciated. Teachers who teach detracked classes are part of an important reform, and they should be publicly acknowledged for their dedication to providing all students with the opportunity to excel.

Concluding Thoughts on the Politics of Detracking

We have learned firsthand that it is possible to overcome political objections to detracking if there is a shared sense of commitment and a vision that can be clearly articulated. Vigilance is key. Reformers should be wary of opposing alliances, which can quickly build and gain momentum, but they should do their best to address their concerns. Although such alliances may represent a vocal minority, they should be heard and acknowledged.

Courage and patience are valuable assets, but nothing can take the place of being prepared. Hard work follows the initial plans for detracking, and school leaders must be able to articulate what will change when the reform begins: Curriculum must be revised or developed anew; teaching strategies must be improved; new support systems must be put in place. In short, if detracking reform is to go forward, it is critical that you keep all promises you make. The next chapter provides guidance on how schools can successfully meet the challenge of implementing the best curriculum for all learners so that achievement increases and equity and excellence become a reality.

5

....

Professional Development for Equitable Practices

In order to effectively teach all students in detracked classes, teachers need professional development that will help them replace traditional practices with differentiated instructional techniques. In addition, such professional development must keep its eye on the prize, namely, an increase in learning for all students. Weiss and Pasley (2006) reviewed and synthesized a full decade of research on effective professional development, identifying essential programmatic features that result both in change in teachers' practice and sustained gains in student achievement. According to the authors, the research indicates that professional development should do the following:

- Be grounded in research
- Align with curriculum, standards, and assessments
- Be intensive and sustained over time, with follow-up support
- Focus on student learning
- Actively engage teachers
- Provide time for teachers and administrators to collaborate within a school and across the district
- Nurture teacher leadership by tapping the expertise of teachers
- Foster the participation and support of principals

Professional development for detracking with vigilance requires nothing less. Our district's multiyear professional development initiatives from 2000 to the present day include these features and focus on the consistent use of data to modify and adjust the initiative. Our professional development has been guided by short- and long-term goals that maintain a vision for student learning. If schools are to give each child an opportunity to be successful, then instructional techniques need to be examined, modified, and refined.

Building a Professional Development Program

When our district began to change the structure of its instructional program from multiple levels of courses taught in homogeneous classes to an "honors for all" model in heterogeneous classes, the curriculum was redesigned with clear goals for students in mind. Teachers wanted students to become deep, independent readers, writers, and thinkers. At the same time, the district needed to establish instructional goals for staff. All adults, including administrators, would have to acquire the knowledge and skills needed to design and implement student-centered lessons that focus on the deep understandings that distinguish high-track curriculum. The professional development plan was designed using student achievement data from prior assessments, an analysis of the skills needed for success in IB courses, and research on effective instructional strategies in heterogeneous classes.

When you detrack a school, team effort is required. Therefore, it is critical that all educators be included in the professional development process. We suggest that sessions include grade-level and content area teachers, building administrators, central office curriculum administrators, and support staff such as special education, academic support, and ESL teachers. Guidance counselors, who often explain the program to parents, should also be included when appropriate. Administrators must attend these sessions to attest to the importance of the activity, to deepen their understanding of the knowledge and skills needed in the classroom, and to strengthen the learning community by building consensus for continuous improvement (Weiss & Pasley, 2006).

The research on professional development is clear—there is no "quick fix" for changing instructional practice. Therefore, our curriculum office committed to an incremental, long-term approach to professional development (Robb, 2000). Our district goals were twofold: to infuse constructivist principles and reading and writing into each curriculum, and to differentiate instruction.

Incorporating Constructivism in Detracked Classes

The belief that learning is an individual, active process is at the heart of the learning theory of constructivism, first proposed by John Dewey and refined by such researchers as Jean Piaget, Lev Vygotsky, and Howard Gardner (see Vermette et al., 2001). Although all classrooms would benefit from the implementation of constructivist principles, in the detracked classroom, active processing is essential. The quick-paced, "present and move on" philosophy, whereby the teacher covers material and expects the learner to absorb it, is deadly in a classroom where students' processing speeds and ways of learning vary. Constructivism is not only for students who need the time to ponder, however. Until its recent popular revival, constructivist teaching thrived in gifted and talented programs (Vermette et al., 2001). Constructivist principles fit perfectly with the philosophy of an enriched educational experience for all students, including high achievers.

Learning to develop constructivist lessons is not easy. In most cases, teachers gravitate toward the methodology by which they were taught, making it very difficult to change traditional teaching practices (Andrews, 2007). Consciously or unconsciously, teachers remember the "telling and showing" teaching that they were exposed to during their schooling, and they replicate that behavior in their own classrooms. In addition, the pressure of high-stakes testing often results in teachers anxiously attempting to cover everything that might be on the test. Conscientious educators are reluctant to use strategies that sacrifice breadth for depth for fear that their students will not be adequately prepared for external examinations. For all of the above reasons and more, the implementation of constructivist teaching strategies takes time and practice.

Because the same constructivist principles that apply to student learning also apply to adult learning, our district chose to create a professional development program that would be multiyear, personalized, and respectful of the needs of teachers (Garrity & Burris, 2007). This chapter delineates the features of that program, which helped our teachers move from traditional practices used in tracked classes to differentiated practices appropriate for heterogeneous classes.

Maximizing Time for Teacher Learning

Professional conversations that allow for thoughtful dialogue are key to the success of a sweeping educational reform such as detracking. The difficult issue is finding the time in a teacher's or administrator's busy day for such conversation and reflection. One must balance the time necessary for productive long-term professional learning with the constraints of teachers' contracts and the hectic schedules of administrators. Our schools have arranged and rearranged professional development sessions to honor these constraints and minimize the loss of instructional time while keeping to a reasonable budget for the activities. The district's model combines different kinds of professional growth opportunities. While some opportunities are mandated, others are teacher-designed and directed. Activities in the program include customized superintendent's conference days, test-scoring sessions, after-school workshops and collegial circles, professional period sessions, out-of-district conferences, and an optional professional plan for tenured teachers in lieu of formal classroom observations.

Professional development that is led by a combination of outside and in-house experts combines new thinking with school expertise. Our district employs outside consultants on a multiyear basis and requires that they provide high-level, intellectually stimulating workshops based on the district's agenda, demonstrate strategies in the classroom, and observe teachers practicing these strategies. Such observations help the consultants understand the unique characteristics of a detracked school. Consultants must be aware of, and agree with, the district's philosophy and culture (Robb, 2000). We also tap the expertise of our own teachers and administrators to facilitate workshops, thus developing in-house consultants who are available to us every school day. This practice also supports the development of shared leadership among teachers.

Superintendent's Conference Days

A sustained, ongoing professional learning model (Darling-Hammond & McLaughlin, 1995), supported by modeling and collectively solving curriculum and instructional problems, is the foundation for redesigning and improving instruction. The state of New York allows schools to have four superintendent's conference days each school year. Our Board of Education designated one conference day for the first day of school, allowing the remaining three days to be customized based on the instructional needs of the district, school, or individual teacher. This new plan provides the latitude to customize full or partial days of targeted professional development by grade level, department, building, interdisciplinary teams, and cross-building teams. Such sessions provide teachers, teaching assistants, and administrators with needed time for professional conversations to discuss important issues, analyze test data, identify student achievement goals, practice new strategies, examine student work, collaborate, and reflect.

Test-Scoring Sessions

During the past decade, researchers have come to recognize and value the importance of using student achievement data in the professional development process (Gandal & McGiffert, 2003). Even scoring exams can provide an opportunity for professional development. No Child Left Behind mandates English language arts (ELA) and mathematics assessments in grades 3 through 8. Although these exams have placed a great burden on schools and students, we have made use of the scoring sessions as an opportunity for professional learning. For example, all 3rd grade teachers, reading teachers, special education teachers, a building principal, and a district curriculum administrator participate in scoring the 3rd grade ELA tests. Rather than mechanically rushing through the scoring, we take the time to analyze questions, share exemplary responses, identify patterns in responses, plan follow-up lessons, and share best practices. Teachers view these sessions as a productive use of their time that will enhance their classroom practice.

After-School Workshops and Collegial Circles

Our teachers' contract requires that each teacher participate in either 16 (veteran teachers) or 20 (new teachers) hours of professional training after school. These sessions include both mandated and teacher-selected workshops. In mandated workshops, teachers learn how to develop effective lessons for detracked classes. We schedule two-hour sessions across the school year so that teachers have the opportunity to incorporate what they have learned in their classroom, and then rejoin their colleagues for reflection and further learning. Teachers, like students, need time to construct meaning and integrate new learning.

Teachers may also fulfill their own professional training requirements by selecting a workshop from a district catalog that includes an array of teacher-taught sessions, collegial circles, and workshops outside of the district. Collegial circles, sometimes referred to as professional learning teams, are quite common and focus on an in-depth study of a curriculum topic, on instructional strategies, or on an analysis of student work. The collegial circles provide teachers with a learner-centered experience that maximizes their prior knowledge, interests, and strengths (Sather & Barton, 2006). The team submits a final report that is shared with grade-level or department staff, thus further increasing the benefit of the study to the entire grade level, department, or school.

Professional Periods

The middle and high schools have a nine-period day, which includes a professional period that may be used for parent conferences and professional discussions. As a follow-up to staff development on writing in the content areas, the high school decided to use the professional period for analysis of student writing. Although the 40-minute period initially seemed too short for productive professional work, by the second session, when teachers better understood the goal of the period, the time proved quite productive.

Teachers were grouped by department based on a common professional period. The sessions facilitated cross–grade-level discussions and the sharing of insights regarding student writing. Working with a literacy consultant, teachers initially reviewed the purpose of writing, the use of the writing conference, and rubrics for assessing written work. Using rubrics from Culham's 6 +1 Traits of Writing (2003), teachers developed a shared perspective of good writing and a common assessment vocabulary to provide meaningful feedback to students. Teachers varied in terms of the trait choice to assess, based on the intent of the assignment and the type of writing. For example, science teachers initially focused on lab reports analyzing two traits—organization and format. They then focused on assessing lab report conclusions. Finally, they discussed the evaluation of the quality of writing, asking these questions:

- Do the *ideas* show insights?
- Is the student's *voice* engaging?
- Is the *word choice* precise?

Each group met for three cycles, with each session proving to be more beneficial as teachers applied the rubrics with their students. The teachers worked in groups of two or three so that the literacy consultant could monitor and adjust the instruction based on their individual needs.

Professional Plans

A tenured teacher, individually or with a partner or a group, may opt to participate in a professional plan in lieu of formal observation by an administrator. Each year the district provides a list of acceptable instructional goals for professional study. Teachers submit a plan to their building administrator identifying the goal, objectives, and activities that will comprise their plan. If accepted and approved at the district level, the building administrator monitors the progress of the plan through informal conferences with the teacher. Teachers submit a written report documenting their activities, which is reflected in their summative evaluation for the year. This option provides another opportunity for teachers to personalize their professional learning based on their needs and encourages collaboration and dialog with colleagues.

As mentioned earlier, learning to design lessons for detracked classes is challenging and cannot be accomplished overnight. We strongly encourage detracking schools to develop a culture in which professional learning is the norm. In such schools, each teacher's classroom is a laboratory for learning, and teachers have the opportunity to observe consultants or colleagues modeling lessons. Teachers need the precious commodity of time to work with their department or grade-level colleagues to increase their content area knowledge, share successful lessons and instructional materials, and learn from each other (Garrity, 2004).

Developing New Teachers

School districts have a unique opportunity—and, we believe, an obligation—to educate new staff beyond their formal schooling and prior experiences. This is especially true in a detracked school. For teachers to be able to meet the needs of all learners, they must be able to use effective instructional strategies that complement the philosophy that all students deserve access to high-quality curriculum and instruction.

Based on a comprehensive study of five school districts, the National Commission on Teaching and America's Future (NCTAF) found that the cost of teacher turnover in the districts drained financial and professional resources, thus undermining the districts' ability to close the achievement gap. With an estimated 46 percent of new teachers leaving the profession during their first five years, the savings gained by decreasing teacher turnover can offset the investment in a comprehensive orientation program for new teachers (NCTAF, 2007).

The New Teacher Institute

In our district, we conduct a five-day New Teacher Institute for new teachers each August, and we follow up with a minimum of 20 hours of activities during the year. The school district and our Teacher Center cosponsor the institute, and a team of teachers and administrators plan the daily activities. District personnel lead four of the days; the fifth day typically features a national speaker focused on literacy across the curriculum. The New Teacher Institute develops a community of learners and reflects a philosophy of professional development that permeates the district.

The superintendent of schools, William H. Johnson, welcomes staff at the district's New Teacher Institute. He delineates the district's goal to provide all students, regardless of their academic, economic, or ethnic background, with the knowledge and skills that will enable them to obtain a Regents diploma, participate in the International Baccalaureate program, complete pre-calculus or calculus, and after high school, finish a college program. He speaks of detracking and how that has helped us achieve these goals. He continuously reiterates that there should be no gaps for poor, minority, or special education students, noting that the district has an ethical obligation to "level the playing field" for learners who have fewer resources at home. As he challenges the staff to work toward this goal, he assures them of the district's full support in this endeavor and of the importance of each professional in the process. He makes it clear that he believes in each student's ability to succeed. Through this introduction, he begins to shape and develop the expectations of new teachers.

Every professional staff member, whether a teacher or an administrator, receives common training in lesson planning and the essential elements of effective instruction in heterogeneous classes. These sessions immerse new teachers in various instructional strategies that are successful in detracked classrooms, such as Think-Pair-Share, jigsaw, and cooperative groups. The facilitators carefully design their lessons to model differentiated instruction. Teachers receive instruction and practice in how to enhance student motivation, increase learning retention, and ensure active student participation.

In any class, but especially in a heterogeneous class, a teacher must divide the lesson into short segments, allow the students to process the information, and check for understanding before moving on in the lesson. We teach new teachers how to provide a summary at different points in the lesson and encourage students to express their learning in their own words so they can adequately form concepts and apply skills.

The development of student reading and writing skills across the curriculum is critical in a school in which all learners are expected to meet high learning standards. Teachers need to learn specific strategies to make reading materials accessible to all students. Laura Robb, a nationally renowned literacy author, participates in the New Teacher Institute and leads follow-up workshops with all staff. She immerses teachers in activities that challenge and inform their teaching practices in reading and writing.

Using authentic instructional materials, teachers reflect on the reading strategies that they use with their students before reading, during reading, and after reading. They then expand their knowledge by practicing additional reading strategies. Teachers preview, connect, and predict using pre-reading strategies such as examining graphics, pictures, boldface words, and headings. Reading strategies designed to reach all learners include the following:

• *Making connections.* Teach students to build new understandings by bringing their knowledge and experience and linking what they read with similar situations, personal experiences, world events, and other text material.

• *Visualization strategies.* Teach students to create a picture in their mind, record the image in their notebook, or describe the picture to a partner.

• *Questioning or monitoring comprehension.* Teach students to identify what is understood and what is confusing through reading, rereading, asking questions, and retelling.

• *Inference-making.* Teach students to understand relationships by examining, for example, dialog, decisions, and conflicts in the text to deepen their understanding of it and determine any unstated meaning.

These strategies go well beyond answering textbook questions. Students must learn how to read closely to clarify meaning, make connections, and deepen their understanding of text. Ms. Robb teaches new teachers how to incorporate a journal or learning log, which can be used throughout the process to note words that are difficult, record questions that arise during and after reading, describe connections with the text, and identify inferences. Teachers receive additional instruction in other reading and writing techniques, such as the following:

• Teacher-provided sentence starters as a reference for journal writing (I never knew _____; I'd like to learn more about _____.)

• Strategies to enhance student test-taking skills in multiple-choice comprehension questions, writing in response to documents, and making inferences to respond to more complex questions

• The use of graphic organizers for pre-reading, vocabulary development, text analysis, and comprehension

• Techniques to identify structural patterns in a text, enabling students to understand the text better and comprehend it at a higher level (Robb, 2006)

Balanced Literacy and Constructivist Practices

New teachers continue their professional learning throughout the school year. One follow-up activity to the New Teacher Institute is a full-day workshop on using the balanced literacy model for reading and writing in the content areas.

Literacy consultant Dale Worsley uses a constructivist approach with teachers to model the instructional practices that are most effective in heterogeneous classes. Teachers examine, analyze, and identify text; engage in writing activities; and review techniques learned at the New Teacher Institute. They are asked to practice the same literacy techniques that their students will use when reading and writing nonfiction. With each activity, teachers are asked to employ the strategic reading strategy of making connections. Sometimes this is done explicitly by selecting a line from the passage with which the reader makes a personal connection. At other times, it is done implicitly through a natural extension of discussion and interaction.

Directed free writes flow through the day to allow teachers to experience the many uses of this technique. Directed free writes for a defined period (usually five minutes) awaken student thinking, allow regular practice responding to a targeted question, and provide time for sharing and reflection. Figure 5.1 provides more information about the uses of directed free writes.

FIGURE 5.1
────────

Directed Free Writes

Directed free writes are a powerful technique that build vocabulary and writing skills in the content areas. Students write for three minutes, then share for two minutes. The chart lists ways to use this technique in the classroom.

When	Why	How	Example	Share
Start of a unit	To determine prior knowledge	Open-ended question	8th grade social studies Civil War unit: "Is war a necessity?"	Tally the opinions on chart paper, with each student contributing one key word to represent his or her opinion.
Midpoint of unit	To assess understanding	Open-ended question	"Could the North or South have avoided the war? Why or why not?"	Divide class based on opinion. Record reasons on chart paper.
End of unit	To assess student growth	Open-ended question	"Was the Civil War a necessity?"	Tally the opinions on chart paper, with each student contributing one key word to represent his or her opinion. Compare to the original chart.
Start of a lesson	To assess readiness for lesson	Key vocabulary words	8th grade math: "Relate the words factor, greatest common factor, and integer."	Share with a partner by reading words verbatim. Select a sentence from the partner's writing to share with the class.

(continues)

FIGURE 5.1
———
Directed Free Writes (*continued*)

When	Why	How	Example	Share
End of a lesson or after group work	To individually assess key objective of lesson	Exit card	"Factor: $x^2 + x - 20$ and explain your answer using the terms factor, greatest common factor, and integer."	Teacher reads after class to determine understanding of process and vocabulary.
Start of a writing piece	To spark interest in writing	Response to a quote	6th grade English: "After reading 'The Cay,' respond to the following quote by Martin Luther King Jr.: 'We may have come on different ships, but we're in the same boat now.'"	Read words verbatim to a partner. Select a sentence from the partner's writing to record in large letters on a sheet of paper and post.
Next writing class	To expand student thinking	Select one of the posted sentences	"Using another student's sentence as your opening line, respond to the same quote."	Copy each original and second piece of writing so that each student can compare the original use of the sentence with the second version.

During the literacy workshop, teachers participate in a variety of structures that can be used to differentiate instruction, such as a jigsaw activity. Using a jigsaw model, teachers work in expert groups to read and analyze nonfiction text. To model the incorporation of learning styles, the nonfiction text is presented in a variety of ways: a biographical note, a picture book, a drama, and a mathematically based article. Each group reads the assigned text and creates an oral presentation with a visual component (and, if they desire, a theatrical component) to teach the group the information represented in their text. Each teacher must have a role in the presentation, and teachers practice listening and accountability strategies as they attend to each presentation (Worsley et al., 2003).

Teachers also partake in a brief writer's workshop to experience the different phases of writing from draft to published piece. From the beginning of the workshop to the end, the facilitator models practices that are constructivist and appropriate for heterogeneous classes.

The constructivist approach and use of differentiated materials modeled in the workshops give new teachers experience with both content and instructional approaches that will serve them (and their students) in their heterogeneous classrooms. Each teacher receives a binder filled with materials for teaching reading and writing in the content areas, such as graphic organizers, mind maps, character charts, explanations of protocols for instructional strategies, and professional references.

Using Achievement Data to Improve Instruction

Student achievement data provide invaluable insights into curriculum and instruction. Detracked schools need to carefully review data to ensure that low achievers are not being left behind and high achievers are still being challenged. Our district uses data not only to retrospectively demonstrate a program's success but also to drive professional development. The administrators and teachers review overall achievement, specific item analyses, and cohort growth for all external assessments. Professional development sessions are then constructed to incorporate this analysis, not as a "test prep" approach but rather as a dynamic one designed to inspire strategic instruction.

An ELA K–8 Example

It is typical for schools to focus on errors made by low achievers when analyzing achievement scores. However, the errors of high achievers provide an excellent source of data as well. When low achievers miss questions, it may be a reflection of what was taught, how it was taught, or the child's individual learning issues. When high achievers demonstrate a pattern of missed answers, the issue is often the curriculum.

On a recent state language arts assessment, our district's highest-performing 4th and 8th graders had difficulty with reading comprehension when it related to the author's purpose in poetry. Based on these data, the literacy consultant developed full-day workshops for grades 3–8 classroom and support teachers to help them design lessons around the inferential skills necessary to appreciate and understand poetry (Garrity, 2004). Teachers began by listening to and reading sophisticated poems to set the stage for the day's work. Knowing that their writing would be shared with partners, each teacher completed a free write, an open-ended activity, which allowed the writers to open their minds on paper. During the sharing activity, teachers selected the best lines from their partner's writing and combined these lines to compose a collaborative poem. Next, each teacher assessed his or her own experience with poetry in the classroom via a directed free write prompt. As the teachers shared their writing, participants recorded a list of strategies for poetry writing and posted them on flip charts set up throughout the room. Notes from the workshop were distributed to all participants afterward.

After establishing a positive, collaborative tone and acknowledging the poetry strategies used by the staff, coauthor Delia Garrity modeled the analysis and interpretation of the test data using student results from high to low, with a specific item analysis of the questions related to poetry from the state assessments. Teachers offered explanations for the results and recognized the need for alternative instructional strategies.

In response groups of four, teachers analyzed poems in text-based seminars and then worked with partners to determine the author's purpose. Pairs of teachers selected a poem from a group of challenging poems and responded to the following questions:

- What did the poem make you sense? Draw it.
- How did the poem make you feel emotionally? Act it out.
- What did the poem make you think? Write it.
- What was the author's purpose? Write it.

Each pair then wrote a new poem, modeled on the chosen poem, and shared it with the rest of their four-person response group. Based on their statements of author's purpose, the partners revised their work and shared their final piece using art, drama, and writing, further consolidating their learning.

This activity immersed teachers in a model that challenged them intellectually and provided a sound blueprint for classroom instruction. A crucial component of professional learning is that teachers experiment with experiences similar to those of their students to determine the validity of the activity and to establish a comfort level for their own instruction (Floden & McDiarmid, 1994).

The same groups of teachers participated in follow-up activities during the next school year. Using curriculum topics, they wrote poetry in a variety of styles. Here is a sample list poem created by 3rd grade teachers Deirdre Rinn, Ann Ferrara, and Diane Silk in response to a unit on butterflies:

> Butterflies have bright colors: red, orange, and black.
> Butterflies have wings: delicate, quick, and shapely.
> Butterflies have a proboscis: long, curly, and sensitive.

As an extension of these workshops, elementary and middle school teachers participated in a summer curriculum-writing project in which they researched incorporating poetry into the areas of social studies and science. When students read, analyze, and write poetry related to content area subjects, they experience a deeper understanding of the vocabulary and content and improvement in their ability to read and write in the content area (Kane & Rule, 2004).

A Foreign Language Grades 6–10 Example

In addition to individual student data, aggregated data across assessments can provide a rich source of information for professional development. In a detracked system, where high learning goals apply to all children, data from the most challenging assessments provide critical insights. As an example, both our middle and high school students perform exceptionally well on external foreign language state assessments. In 8th grade, 99 percent pass the state proficiency exam, and in 10th grade, 98 percent pass the

Regents exam. In 12th grade, however, students do not fare as well on the IB exams in Spanish and French.

Foreign language staff in middle and high school had to address the issue. Our students performed at high levels on state assessments, but what else could we do to enhance the curriculum to better prepare them for the challenges of IB? The teachers' initial reaction was defensive. They did not recognize their connection to student performance in grades 11 and 12. However, if the goal were to hold all students to high learning standards, as exemplified by the assessments of the IB, then IB assessments would need to influence language instruction in grades 6–10. The vast majority of South Side High School students take foreign language in the upper grades, and there is only one heterogeneously grouped level from the beginning to the end of foreign language instruction. Taking a long-range look at the district's goal of providing access to the IB diploma (for which foreign language study is required) reminds teachers of their critical role in achieving this goal (Floden & McDiarmid, 1994).

The professional development sessions that addressed this specific goal in foreign language included the following components:

• A half-day pullout session with the literacy consultant, teachers of grades 6 to 8, the middle school principal, and the curriculum coordinator to examine test data, the present curriculum, and the *Middle Years IB Principles for Language B* (MYP IB).*

• A full-day session with the literacy consultant, all foreign language teachers grades 6 to 8, the middle school principal, a high school assistant principal, the curriculum coordinator, one Regents/IB Spanish teacher, and one Regents/IB French teacher to explore the requirements of the IB, the areas where students perform well, and the areas where they struggle.

• A full-day session with all foreign language teachers grades 6 to 8, the middle school principal, and the curriculum coordinator to determine the specific changes to be made to the curriculum in grades 6 to 8 as a result of the previous session.

---

*The *Middle Years Program of the International Baccalaureate* is a whole-school, portfolio-driven program designed for students ages 11–16. Specifically, the *Language B* program of the IB requires students to actively engage in an in-depth study of the target language through immersion in various formative and summative tasks of reading, writing, listening, and speaking.

By design, the initial session did not include staff from the high school. The middle school teachers needed time to reflect on their accomplishments, understand their role in helping students be successful in IB foreign language classes, and examine the structure and content of their curriculum. Surprisingly, the teachers in grades 6 and 7 quickly acknowledged that they had the time to teach more content and to teach the present content at a deeper level. Eighth grade teachers noted that they did not have a substantial amount of extra time, given the present configuration of their curriculum. We reviewed the core MYP IB, and teachers identified both the components included in their curriculum and those that were absent. Teachers realized just how much they relied on the textbook for their instructional approach to the curriculum and explored other literacy strategies to enhance students' experience. The group noted the differences between the performance levels of reading, writing, listening, and speaking as compared with the level of skill expected of students taking the MYP IB language courses.

Using the backwards planning model of curriculum design, as described in Chapter 3, the joint session with middle and high school teachers and administrators focused on the requirements of the IB program. The high school teachers distributed samples of the IB assessments for reading, writing, listening, and speaking. This helped the middle school teachers understand the high level of performance required of high school students. The teachers then examined the New York State Regents exam administered in grade 10 and identified the significant differences between it and the IB exam. High school teachers discussed the reading, writing, listening, and speaking experiences that graduating middle school students should have in order to allow the high school teachers to enrich the 9th and 10th grade courses and better prepare students for the IB assessment.

The third session was dedicated to revising the middle school curriculum. Teachers expanded the original goal of the middle school program—the successful completion of the state proficiency exam in foreign language—to include the broader goal of increasing the depth and breadth of their program. They wanted to help students become better readers, writers, listeners, and speakers of a second language. Teachers examined and revised each resource and assessment tool as well as the themes, cultural study, vocabulary, and grammatical structures to address their new goal. Students would now engage in presentations, including interviews and debates based on the MYP IB. Such activities would provide the heterogeneously grouped students with a greater variety of ways to demonstrate their language learning. Likewise, the skill of listening would be linked to oral communication with students responding to, for example, interviews, debates, and weather reports. Reading would now include a variety of texts beyond the course textbook including magazines, news articles, and picture books. Writing tasks would be correlated with the oral tasks and also include letter writing and simple essays. The study of culture exposes the students to present-day news in print and video to build awareness and understanding of the perspectives of other cultures where the target language is spoken. In short, the middle-school language program has been transformed from a traditional curriculum to one that is more rigorous and differentiated in task, materials, and assessments. Teachers also applied the balanced literacy model to determine common benchmarks for each grade level.

Multiyear Initiatives for Instructional Practices

Research studies confirm that for a professional development initiative to result in change in teaching practices, the program must be intensive, sustained, and deeply rooted in identified performance goals (Darling-Hammond & McLaughlin, 1995; Robb, 2000; Weiss & Pasley, 2006). If you expect teachers to progress from old practices to new, you cannot depend upon one-shot staff development sessions.

As mentioned in Chapter 1, detracking in our district began as a strategy to meet student achievement goals. Our superintendent set the following performance goals during the past decade: to increase the number of students earning a Regents diploma; to give all students access to calculus by accelerating the study of mathematics; and to increase the number of students taking IB courses and obtaining an IB diploma.

Superintendent Johnson regularly communicates with each constituency group during superintendent's conference days, public Board of

Education meetings, and various parent forums to reiterate these performance goals and to describe the ongoing professional development plans needed to educate staff so that each goal can be achieved. His 22 years as superintendent of the district, coupled with stability in central office and building administration, have substantially increased the successful attainment of district goals (Weiss & Pasley, 2006). We now will detail three multiyear, goal-driven, rigorous initiatives that have substantially effected change in instructional practice in our district. Each one was identified as vital to ensuring that all students could be successful in detracked classes.

Mathematics K–5: Developing Constructivist Practices

In Chapter 3 we described the curriculum change in mathematics at the elementary level undertaken in order to allow all students to complete Mathematics A, the state graduation requirement in mathematics, by the end of 8th grade. This change ensured that all students would be on the path to studying calculus in 12th grade.

The new 5th grade mathematics curriculum, a 6th-grade-level program, uses a constructivist approach and emphasizes deep mathematical thinking, problem solving, and communication. We introduced a similar mathematics program in grades K–4. Because our elementary school teachers were accustomed to a more traditional, text-based approach to mathematics, they needed time to learn and practice a constructivist approach, so we hired a math-implementation teacher who serves as a districtwide professional developer and math coach for the elementary school staff. Prior to each unit of study, the implementation teacher meets with teachers by grade level for a half-day session to review the math content, practice each investigation, and identify ways of differentiating the lessons. She then models lessons in the teachers' classrooms and provides opportunities for team teaching a lesson. She also meets with teachers to answer questions, assists with planning, provides encouragement, and ensures that each teacher has the proper instructional materials. This extensive professional development model, which focuses on math content and instructional strategies, proved to be the vital component in the successful implementation of our K–8 mathematics curriculum. Providing all students with a rich, well-taught curriculum that differentiates learning prepares them for challenging math in 8th grade and beyond.

Reading and Writing in the Content Areas K–12

As we examined student performance across the areas of curricula, we found that students were struggling with questions that required critical reading and writing skills. Although students understood a specific concept, when that concept was embedded in text, many students had difficulty reading and interpreting the question or task. If all students were to assume the challenges of the IB program, we needed to change how we taught reading and writing.

To enhance skills in all learners, the district designed a five-year, K–12 professional development plan focusing on reading and writing across the content areas. The plan emphasized that every teacher was responsible for literacy instruction; articulated the vision that all students can be deep readers, writers, and thinkers in all subject areas; and highlighted the types of reading and writing skills that would be necessary for students to realize this vision. A synopsis of the plan is shown in Figure 5.2.

All teachers, building administrators, and central office administrators participated in these activities. The activities overlapped throughout the years based on the availability of staff, the introduction of new staff, and the integration of curriculum projects based on the goals.

During the first year of the initiative, the district adopted and adapted the balanced literacy model. Teachers received training in the model in grade-level groups at the elementary level and departmental groups at the middle school and high school levels. In the second year, our consultant used adult-level reading selections to immerse teachers in specific content literacy instruction from a constructivist perspective.

During the third year of the literacy initiative, a "Teachers as Writers" workshop engaged teachers in the writing process, addressed the writing standards in each content area, and nurtured interdisciplinary and inter-grade collaboration. During the full-day workshop, teachers and administrators—including the superintendent—followed the writing process, from concept maps to drafts that were critiqued by a response group. After

FIGURE 5.2

Reading and Writing in the Content Areas: A Five-Year Initiative

Year	Content	Process	Participants	Facilitator	Time Allotment
1	Balanced Literacy	Immersion in reading/writing workshop	All teachers districtwide	Dale Worsley, consultant	Full-day workshop; 2 hours after school
2	Strategic Reading Strategies	Using sophisticated text, teachers apply strategies	All teachers districtwide	Dale Worsley and Laura Robb, consultants	Full-day workshop; 2 hours after school
3	Teachers as Writers	Immersion in writing workshop	All teachers districtwide	Dale Worsley, consultant	Full-day workshop; 2 hours after school
4	Exit Writing Project/ Nonfiction Writing	Each building determines writing goals by grade level	All teachers grades K–8	Building design teams and Laura Robb, consultant	Two half-day workshops; two 2-hour after-school sessions
	Student Writing	Collaborative assessment	High school teachers	Dale Worsley, consultant	Three professional periods
5	Curriculum Assessment	Designing rigorous common assessments	Middle school: English, science, social studies, foreign language	Dale Worsley, consultant	Two half-day workshops; two 2-hour after-school sessions

the workshop, teachers finalized their piece, either alone or with members of their response group. Approximately one month later, the group met after school to share a final version of their writing. These pieces were collected and published in an anthology. Teachers were actively engaged in these sessions as they reflected on the process as well as the written product. It was a powerful experience. When the superintendent spends a day and an afternoon in such a workshop with staff, the message is clear: The goal of literacy is paramount.

After this experience, teachers met by building and by grade level or department to determine the applications of writing goals within their curriculum and to design specific writing activities that would lead to a culminating 5th or 8th grade project. The culminating student project at the high school level was the IB extended essay.

A building design team from one of the elementary schools developed a comprehensive matrix that delineated the grade-level writing skills required for students to successfully produce their targeted writing genre (see Figure 5.3 for an extract of this matrix). The team linked the works of grade-level authors with writing strategies and portfolio pieces. For example, while reading a book by Cynthia Rylant, students in 2nd grade focused on correctly using possessives and using stronger, sensory words in their writing. The product was a small-moment personal narrative for their portfolio.

Grade-level teams use the matrix as a guide to plan lessons, assess student writing, and adjust instruction based on the learning needs of each student. This personalized approach to writing allows teachers to address the range of writing skill development in their heterogeneous classes. Teachers also met in mixed grade-level groups to study samples of student work, assess the structure of the writing lessons that produced that work, and improve the lesson design as needed.

The middle school's exit writing project focused on the research process. The final student products included both written and oral components and were developed in the content areas as in-depth studies of a curriculum topic rather than add-ons. Four half-day and after-school workshops allowed each group of teachers, along with a building administrator, a central office administrator, and the building library media specialist, to develop the structure and goals of the project, a timeline for periodic checks of student work, note-taking forms, assessment requirements, and grading rubrics.

Middle school students' projects take multiple forms. In 6th grade science, each student researches a personal question that piques his or her curiosity about the human body. After reading *The Giver* by Lois Lowry, 7th grade English students complete research on memories using primary

FIGURE 5.3

Grade-Level Matrix of Writing Skills

Grade Level	K	1	2	3
Authors	Lois Ehlert Eric Carle Donald Crews Frank Asch Denise Fleming	Kevin Henkes Leo Leonni Robert Munsch Charlotte Zolotow	Tomie DePaola Mem Fox Vera B. Williams Cynthia Rylant	Johanna Hurwitz Patricia Reilly Giff Eve Bunting Beverly Cleary
Skills	• Letter identification • Letter sounds • Letter formation • Forming words/inventive spelling and conventional spelling (Orton) • Sentence structure—spacing • Simple sentences • Capitals • Action words (verbs) • Describing words (adjectives) • Periods • Question marks • Exclamation points • Revising—insert ∧	• Review letter sounds • Letter blends • Sentence structure • Nouns • Verbs • Adjectives • Adverbs • Setting • Problem/solution • Capitalization—proper nouns, months, places, beginning of sentence • Periods, question marks, exclamation points • Commas—date, series of 3	• Spelling patterns • Compound words • Homonyms/homographs • Root/base words • Suffix and prefix • Capitalization • Ending punctuation • Comma use • Quotation marks • Nouns, verbs, adjectives • Pronouns, adverbs • Possessives • Subject/predicate • Plurals/irregular plurals	• Spelling patterns • Homonyms/homographs • Root/base words • Suffix and prefix • Capitalization • Ending punctuation • Comma use • Quotation marks • Nouns, verbs • Adjectives—superlative, comparative • Pronouns, adverbs • Possessives • Identifying articles • Subject/predicate • Plurals/irregular plurals

(continues)

FIGURE 5.3

Grade-Level Matrix of Writing Skills (*continued*)

Grade Level	K	1	2	3
Skills		• Revising—insert ^ • Editing—spelling, capitalization, punctuation • Conventional spelling (Orton)		
Genres	• Journal writing (personal and content-based) • Poetry (list and free verse) • Letter writing (friendly and invitation) • Creative writing • Literary response	• Journal writing (personal and content-based) • Poetry (list, free verse, and rhyming) • Persuasive writing (opinion) • Personal narrative • Creative writing • Literary response • Note taking • Research	• Journal writing (personal and content-based) • Letter writing • Postcards • Poetry • Retellings • Descriptive paragraphs • Memoir • Point of view • Creative writing • Directed narratives • Expository • Literary response • Compare/contrast	• Journal writing (personal and content-based) • Personal narratives • Directed response writing • Persuasive essays (facts and opinions) • Expository • Fantasy stories • Document-based questions (DBQ) • Compare/contrast • Poetry • Research

Writing strategies	• Engage in the basic process of writing to improve content, variety, and accuracy (prewrite, draft, revise, edit, publish) • Work independently and cooperatively with peers (response groups, conferencing)	• Beginning, middle, and end in writing • Note taking • Graphic organizers • Engage in the basic process of writing to improve content, variety, and accuracy (prewrite, draft, revise, edit, publish) • Work independently and cooperatively with peers (response groups, conferencing)	• Graphic organizers • Home run sentences • Single paragraphs of 4–6 sentences—topic sentences, details, closing (guided) • Use of editor's marks • Multiparagraph form (guided) • Engage in the basic process of writing to improve content, variety, and accuracy (prewrite, draft, revise, edit, publish)	• Graphic organizers • Paragraph structure • Engage in the basic process of writing to improve content, variety, and accuracy (prewrite, draft, revise, edit, publish) • Work independently and cooperatively with peers (response groups, conferencing)
Portfolio pieces	• Illustrated story • Writing for real reason piece • Small-moment personal narrative • Conventions of written language piece • Revision piece • Author's study piece • Nonfiction • Poetry	• Literary response • Personal narrative • Authors' study story • Nonfiction • Letter • Poetry • Problem/solutions	• Descriptive paragraph • Memoir • Postcards • Expository piece • Poetry • Creative writing	• Personal narrative • Directed response writing • Fantasy story • Persuasive essay

Source: Tricia Bock, Kristi Bonino, and Anne DeFranza, Riverside Elementary School, Rockville Centre, New York.

sources from a given time period, conduct interviews, listen to guest speakers, write a paper, and reflect on the research process. During the study of westward expansion, 8th grade students answer the question, "Westward expansion: boom or bust?" by assuming the role of a person at that time in history, by conducting research from that perspective, and then by collaborating with a group of students. Finally, students present an oral argument with creative visuals. These school-designed projects are linked to the curriculum and require students to do independent research. Students learn to develop a bibliography, adhere to a timeline, make an oral presentation, and reflect in writing on the process.

As teachers across content areas and grade levels implement strategies and projects, the instructional model has shifted from teachers assuming that students have necessary reading and writing skills to lessons that include instruction in specific literacy strategies in the content area. Students learn to talk about their reading and writing in order to connect concepts across disciplines. Classroom observations indicate that students regularly engage in directed free writes, text annotation and analysis, the writing process, and Think-Pair-Share activities.

Differentiated Instruction K–12

In 1999, our district adopted a schoolwide enrichment model (Renzulli & Reis, 1997) that uses the classroom curriculum as the basis for explorations, extensions, and applications. The elementary classroom teachers plan and implement enrichment activities with the STELLAR teacher, the professional in each building responsible for coordinating the inclusive gifted and talented program.

When the district changed the elementary GT program from one that was selective to one that is inclusive, STELLAR teachers and one of the elementary school principals spent a week at a summer institute sponsored by Renzulli to acquire background knowledge on the schoolwide enrichment model and write a curriculum for the program. During the first year, elementary school principals and their teachers also participated in a series of workshops on differentiating instruction. Drawing on the work of Howard Gardner (1993), teachers broadened their understanding of students' multiple intelligences and learned how to include them when planning units of study. Teachers also incorporated the early research of Carol Ann Tomlinson (1999) as they assessed the content of the grade-level curriculum, teaching strategies, and expectations for student work. We built upon this knowledge over the next three years using Tomlinson's (2001) more recent work, designing lessons in small segments with checks for understanding and processing of the information. Other differentiating strategies that teachers easily incorporated into their lessons include the following:

- Homework options aligned with learning profiles
- Student choice in projects based on multiple intelligences
- Varied journal prompts
- Differentiated spelling words
- Think-Pair-Share by interest and learning profile
- Graphic organizers and flip books for note taking, vocabulary, and test review
- Concept maps represented graphically or pictorially
- Active processing activities: stop and jot, Think-Pair-Share, and exit cards
- Flexible grouping

Our middle and high school teachers also underwent professional development in differentiated instruction. Teachers shared their experiences with both building and districtwide colleagues. They began to generate supplements to curriculum documents that reflected ways of differentiating processes and products while still maintaining a high standard of learning for all students.

We have learned that it is easy to misunderstand the practical applications of differentiation. At times, teachers and administrators thought that differentiation was just another word for in-class ability grouping. However, detracking and setting high learning standards for all means that each student must achieve the goals of the lesson or unit. The *curriculum* is never differentiated, and each student in the end must be successful on the required local, state, and international assessments. We believe that differentiated instruction allows for multiple approaches to teaching content; it is not about *what* you teach but *how* you teach.

We continued professional development in this vital area. Beginning in 2002, differentiated instruction strategies were blended into the reading and writing initiative, as previously described. As 9th and 10th grade courses became heterogeneous, with all students learning at the honors level, more professional learning was needed.

A professional development team composed of the high school principal (coauthor Carol Corbett Burris) and two high school teachers (English teacher Christine Brown and art teacher Keith Gamache) researched the literature on differentiating instruction and designed and facilitated five two-hour professional development sessions for high school staff. Teachers and administrators were grouped in interdisciplinary study groups of 25 with an even distribution of newer and experienced staff in each group. During the first three sessions, teachers participated in and assessed differentiated lessons based on multiple intelligences, achievement, and interest. The first session focused on multiple intelligences and learning styles. The instructor modeled a differentiated English lesson that incorporated multiple intelligence theory. Based on the results of a learning strength inventory, the facilitator created heterogeneous groups of teachers to learn and practice sophisticated vocabulary. Members of the group completed the task using a strategy that best suited their learning strength: an illustration, a connection described in a journal entry, a poem, a song, or a selected graphic organizer. The group members shared their work with their team members, received feedback, and revised their work. Teachers then "jigsawed" into new groups, in which they learned new vocabulary words using the same intelligence. Teachers reflected on the process and on the lesson design that gave participants responsibility and ownership for their own learning, allowed for multiple paths to the same objective, and developed a community of learners.

In the second session, teachers participated in a mathematics lesson differentiated by achievement levels (see Chapter 6 for the detailed lesson plan). They worked in department-based groups to present the solution to a real-world problem using either a narrative, a sketch, or a graph.

Teachers were regrouped into heterogeneous groups and one math "expert group" to complete the next task. The heterogeneous groups had to solve a problem using a pattern of change while the expert group derived a general equation that could be used to solve all problems. Each group then shared solutions and methods, and the expert group taught the equation to the class. Again, a common objective was reached by multiple means.

The third session focused on differentiation by assessment. This time, teachers and administrators participated in an art lesson. Participants completed various sketching tasks using different entry points: narrational (from a reading) and quantitative (applying ratios). Based on the initial sketches, experimentation with a variety of materials, and modeling by the facilitator, teachers were given a choice of methods to create the final drawing so they could work toward their strength. When used in the classroom, each phase of the sketching lesson becomes part of the assessment, rather than only the final piece, thus allowing students to demonstrate growth within the assignment. The journey is as important as the destination as the students demonstrate their active involvement in the process, construct their own learning, and clearly understand the objective.

At the end of the last two sessions, teachers applied their learning from the three instructional workshops by designing a short differentiated lesson with departmental colleagues and teaching it to the entire study group. Teachers who observed the lessons identified entry points, level of student engagement, types of learning tasks, choice of materials, and assessment tools. Teachers received praise and constructive feedback to assist them in future lesson design and delivery.

Building a Community of Learners

Facilitating a move from the traditional pedagogy of tracked classes to the student-centered pedagogy that is needed for detracking requires a strong, intensive, and sustained professional development program. Teachers and administrators need time to reflect on their own practice, analyze data and curriculum, and actively engage in the process. Threaded through this chapter are examples of teachers and administrators playing the dual roles of student and teacher, with each staff member acting as colleague, learner, and facilitator. The days of teaching in isolation are behind us as each classroom becomes a learning lab and teachers open their minds and their classroom doors. The previous district-based education model, which developed common understandings of goals, curriculum, and effective instruction, has given way to a building-based model of professional communities where teachers and administrators work collaboratively to apply the district's goals and philosophy to ensure a high level of learning for all students (DuFour, DuFour, Eaker, & Many, 2006).

Building Design Teams

Our first professional learning community grew out of professional development in reading and writing in content areas, during which each building created a building design team to implement the learned strategies and ideas from the districtwide training. The team strengthens the implementation model by listening to their colleagues, keeping staff focused on continuous improvement in literacy, and sharing best practices with the other schools.

Staff leadership opportunities expand when teacher expertise is used to plan and facilitate professional development programs. As described in the previous section, members of the high school staff took the lead in teaching differentiated instructional practices. The following year, the same team provided turnkey training to the principal and teacher teams from our middle school and our five elementary schools. Each building team then customized the training based on the instructional needs of their teachers and the learning needs of their students. For example, at Covert Elementary School, Principal Darren Raymar joined teachers Michelle De Martino and Jennifer Guttman in serving as turnkey trainers for the Covert staff. As a result, the building staff shared a common vocabulary and goal. The team's efforts also resulted in teachers developing a deep understanding of how to provide the differentiated learning experiences that helped more Covert students be successful. During the third year, the Covert team trained all new elementary teachers in the district.

Each year ends with teachers contributing their lessons to a districtwide or schoolwide anthology of differentiated lessons.

Lesson Study

New strategies must be nurtured and practiced if they are to survive. High school teachers wanted to continue their collaborative work designing and critiquing differentiated lessons. In response to teacher input, Burris and her high school professional development team, Brown and Gamache, researched the lesson study model and used it to further embed differentiated practice. Lesson study, first practiced by Japanese teachers, is a professional development strategy for creating, examining, and improving lessons with collegial input. It focuses on "clear learning goals for students, a shared curriculum, the support of administrators, and the hard work of teachers striving to make gradual improvements in their practice" (Stigler & Hiebert, 1999, p. 109). This model for professional learning seemed a good fit in that it is based on research, uses a collaborative building-based design, and is practiced in the classroom.

Initially, each high school teacher received a collection of articles to build background knowledge of the lesson study model. The high school design team led an informational session, and then teachers formed collaborative groups of two to four members, based on common preparation periods, to develop a differentiated lesson. During a mutually agreeable time arranged by the building administration, one teacher volunteered to teach the lesson to one of his or her classes while the other team members observed. The team then unpacked the lesson using a rubric to evaluate engagement and participation of students, selection of open-ended materials, questioning strategies, and assessment techniques (see Appendix B for an example of the rubric). It is important to note that the focus of the analysis is on the lesson, not the teacher, as the lesson design is the result of a group effort. After revising the lesson, another member of the group taught while others observed and offered more refinements. Each team completed two cycles of lesson study. The result was twofold: First, teachers developed a collection of differentiated lessons, and second, teachers' understanding of differentiation deepened.

Analyzing Professional Development's Effect on Achievement

What evidence exists that links teacher learning to student achievement? Teacher quality is often mentioned in research as the most significant factor in improving student achievement, accountable for 40 percent of the difference in test scores (Darling-Hammond & Loewenberg-Ball, 1997). Darling-Hammond and Loewenberg-Ball argue that the quality of initial teacher preparation and the continuous education of teachers in content and methodology are central to greater student achievement. When you institute a detracking reform, adult learning is imperative. For students to receive the full benefits of detracking, professional development must be curriculum-based, intensive, and sustained over time with follow-up support. Professional development activities must maintain a focus on stated goals for student achievement and include a regular review of achievement data in order to assess progress and plan future sessions. Districtwide and building-based activities allow for an understanding of the big picture and the unique application of the understanding in each building.

The increases in our district's Regents diploma rate, strong IB results, and other assessment data are a result of making sure that teachers did not have to "go it alone" during the detracking reform. We believe that a strong professional development model, similar to that presented in this chapter, is essential if all students are to be successful learners in detracked classrooms. Would student achievement have increased without professional development, based only on the reconfiguration of courses into heterogeneous classes? We think not. Teachers had to change their frame of reference and practices. Professional development is an investment, not a frivolous expense that can be eliminated from a budget in tough economic times.

At the same time, detracking does not need to be delayed until every teacher is fully trained. In Rockville Centre, professional development occurred as we detracked. Adult learning, just like student learning, cannot occur in a vacuum. Part of our success was due to the fact that teachers could learn and then immediately practice their new knowledge in their heterogeneous classes.

As you reflect on your own professional development program, we suggest that you ask the following questions:

1. What are your long- and short-term goals, and how well would they support a detracking initiative?

2. What skills will your students need to be successful in heterogeneous classes with an enriched curriculum? What assessments might provide the data to answer that question?

3. What building expertise can you draw on, and in what areas might you need outside support?

4. After you begin your detracking reform, how will you train new teachers?

5. How can you maximize time for ongoing adult learning for both teachers and administrators?

In the next chapter, we discuss the implementation of professional development where it matters most—in the classroom.

6

....

Teaching and Learning in the Heterogeneous Classroom

When we began the detracking process in the Rockville Centre School District, there was comparatively little research available on the best methods for teaching heterogeneous classes. We used Madeline Hunter's instructional model—a model we continue to follow for basic lesson development—and encouraged teachers to regularly integrate cooperative learning in their lessons for guided practice. Support classes and extra help provided alternative instruction and extra practice for learners who struggled. During this early phase of detracking, when the lowest track was eliminated and three tracks became two, we were not familiar with practices such as differentiated instruction and constructivism. Even so, students benefited from detracking, and student achievement scores increased.

We now have even more instructional strategies to apply in our schools. Constructivist learning theory and differentiated instruction strategies have provided insights into how we can adjust teaching to meet the needs of diverse learners. New knowledge of learner-centered educational practices has taught us that schools can deliver the promise of meeting the needs of all learners without resorting to ability grouping. By altering our methods of instruction in heterogeneous classes, we can accomplish what tracking never could—excellent educational experiences for all students.

In tracked systems, accountability lies with the learner. When a student does not meet the learning standard of a particular track, he or she is leveled down to an "easier" class. The adults are let off the hook. In detracked schools, accountability lies with the adults, who must create strategies to reach all learners and help them maximize their learning potential. In an age of accountability to the public, leveling students down to the "easy class" can no longer be the solution. And that, we contend, is a step in the right direction.

In many ways, the most difficult phase of detracking is when a school begins to question its assumptions and beliefs about teaching practices. Teachers have to reflect more on their practice and change instruction to meet the needs of diverse learners. Traditional lectures and "chalk and talk" simply will not work. This chapter is our attempt to share what we have learned as teachers who engaged in such reflection and developed effective instruction for heterogeneous classes.

Student-Centered Lessons and Active Learning

Students are not passive vessels into which we pour knowledge. As we teach, learners should actively seek to make connections with prior experiences and negotiate what they are learning with what they have learned before. Learners need time to process concepts and information in order to retain new ideas. Rote learning and "chalk and talk" methodology do little to promote deep understanding for the majority of students.

Traditional Instruction, Tweaked and Transformed

In the preceding chapter, we discussed the intensive and ongoing professional development necessary to help teachers learn how to create lessons that are both constructivist and differentiated. Later in this chapter, we will discuss the implementation and components of such lessons, presenting actual lesson plans and lesson-planning procedures. However, there are strategies that teachers can use to increase active learning in heterogeneous classrooms even within the confines of more traditional lessons.

For example, "chalk and talk" can be more effective if the teacher orally presents concepts or ideas, pauses, and then follows with notes on the overhead or chalkboard. This technique allows students to process the information aurally prior to reading and then writing notes. Well-organized chalkboards, where old concepts are erased before new ones are added and information is presented from left to right, help to prevent confusion for students who have processing difficulties. Writing the lesson objective and the date on the board, and then leaving them on until the end of the lesson, helps students organize their notebooks and better understand the purpose of the lesson. Integrating visuals, using graphic organizers, showing short film clips, using audiotapes, integrating technology, showing models, and performing demonstrations appeal to learners with different talents and strengths.

Teachers can also differentiate materials for guided practice. In our high school, social studies teachers provide materials that match the reading levels of the students in their class. However, each reading packet contains the important content that all students need. Sometimes students work in groups; other times they work alone. Individual conferences focusing on student writing portfolios individualize writing instruction in English and social studies classes.

At the secondary level, read-alouds of novels and nonfiction texts have been replaced by silent reading so that each learner can read at his or her own pace. Their reading is guided by differentiated questions that are discussed afterward. Students with disabilities can listen to books on tape while reading the text. At the elementary level, students move from read-alouds, to interactive reading, to guided reading, and finally to independent reading, based on their skill level.

Not every student needs to do every problem on a math practice sheet—different problems can be assigned to different students, with challenging problems given to high achievers. Prepared cue cards can be quietly passed to students who are struggling with math problems, and extension activities that promote critical thinking and creativity can be provided for students who want extra challenge.

In Figure 6.1, we present strategies that are easy to implement, along with how each strategy complements classrooms in which all learners are included and welcomed. These strategies are not unique or novel, and when they are integrated into lessons, active participation by all students increases. It is important to note that although we suggest differentiating the learning experience, we are not suggesting that schools differentiate standards and outcomes. All students are expected to meet high learning standards. It is our job as educators to vary the strategies so that all can be successful.

Even prior to undergoing any formal training, teachers can work together to identify and expand on the strategies they are already using to meet the needs of diverse learners. Discussions based on the following questions can help facilitate reflective teaching:

• What modalities do teachers generally use when presenting new information? How might a teacher incorporate a modality that's not typically employed?

• What percentage of class time is devoted to teacher talk? What percentage to student talk? How might a teacher increase the involvement of all students?

• Do teachers require all students to do the same thing throughout the class? When and how might a teacher differentiate activities and practice?

• Generally speaking, what is the complexity level of most of the questions that teachers ask? How might a teacher include more higher-level questions? Do teachers use wait time of at least three seconds after asking a question?

Targeted classroom observations can help establish baseline data for all of the above questions and provide teachers with constructive feedback. For example, observations can be focused just on questioning techniques—identify the level of complexity of each question, measure wait time, and "map out" the involvement of students. Such observations can provide teachers with important information about their questioning strategies.

FIGURE 6.1
———
Classroom Strategies to Increase Active Learning

Strategy	Benefit in a Detracked Classroom
Using varied modalities when presenting information	Reinforces content and appeals to the range of learning styles in the classroom
Assigning silent reading with purpose; guided questions may vary	Allows students to read at their own speed
Using five to seven seconds of wait time when asking questions; asking students to jot down a response	Allows high achievers to formulate better-quality answers; students who process information slowly have the opportunity to formulate an answer
Varying the level of questions by difficulty and complexity (Bloom's taxonomy)	Allows for wider participation based on achievement and intelligences
Differentiating materials/practice by skill or achievement level	Moderates the level of challenge according to the achievement of the learner
Using cue cards	Provides scaffolding support during individual or group practice for students who need it
Inviting signaled, choral responses to teacher questions	Checks for understanding across the range of students; allows teacher to adjust instruction, both whole-class and individual
Using paired activities for practice	Allows students to receive peer feedback and elaborate on answers
Offering extension activities	Provides activities for students who require or seek additional challenge
Providing choice in materials or in ways to demonstrate knowledge	Allows students to work with materials and media with which they are most comfortable; increases student motivation
Using exit cards	Provides an individual response to the mastering of the lesson objective
Using the stop and jot technique	Allows students to process and integrate new information

Cooperative Learning in Heterogeneous Classes

Although differentiated instruction is relatively new, cooperative learning strategies are regularly used by teachers and are supported by a substantial body of research. There is a growing amount of literature that provides examples of how carefully crafted cooperative learning experiences can enhance learning in heterogeneous classes (Boaler, 2006; Linchevski & Bilha, 1998).

Cooperative learning allows diversity in a classroom to become a great strength. Teachers can carefully design group membership to complement student talents and interests, helping students to view each other as interdependent learners rather than independent learners in competition. Proponents of cooperative learning (Fore, Riser, & Boon, 2006) cite the work of Piaget and Vygotsky, who proposed that social interactions provide powerful opportunities for student learning, especially from more expert peers. When teachers provide student groups with challenging assignments, cooperative learning can foster productive experiences for all learners, including those with learning disabilities (Fore et al., 2006). Although there are many effective cooperative learning strategies that can be successfully used in a detracked classroom, jigsaw activities are particularly effective, especially when combined with differentiation of materials or presentation. We will discuss how we use the jigsaw in the next section.

Differentiated Instruction

Differentiated instruction is a constructivist approach to teaching and learning that acknowledges that students vary in background knowledge, prior achievement, learning style, interests, and talents. It recognizes that learning occurs in the mind of the learner, and that prior experience and achievement influence what is learned and how it is learned.

When teachers develop a differentiated lesson, their goal is to maximize learning for each individual student in the class. They recognize that active participation is key to learning—when students are engaged in the active processing of new information, they gain a deeper understanding.

In a differentiated lesson, teachers encourage active student participation by providing multiple entry points that help students access the content.

The term "entry point" comes from Howard Gardner's work on multiple intelligences (1993). Gardner identifies five entry points, or pathways, to learning a given topic based on the multiple intelligences that students possess:

- *Narrational.* The teacher uses a story to engage students in the learning.
- *Logical/quantitative.* Logic is used to develop understanding, or the teacher uses numbers or deductive reasoning.
- *Foundational.* Key words and definitions are used.
- *Aesthetic.* The teacher uses musical and visual arts.
- *Experiential.* Students manipulate objects and materials.

According to Gardner, when a teacher includes multiple entry points, possibilities for student learning expand.

In the differentiated classroom, there is more student talk than teacher talk, and more student work than teacher work. Learning is an active process, not a passive one. The teacher is responsible for creating lessons that provide access to meaningful learning tasks that will enable each learner to participate in the lesson more fully. Although the difficulty or complexity of the tasks that students complete may vary, all students contribute essential knowledge that helps the class achieve the learning objective. Lessons can be differentiated by achievement, multiple intelligences, or student interest, or any combination of these three. Below are some examples of differentiated lessons.

A 10th Grade English Language Arts Lesson

As mentioned in Chapter 1, all students at South Side High School take an enriched English language arts (ELA) course in the 10th grade that prepares them for both the International Baccalaureate curriculum in grades 11 and 12 and for the six-hour New York state ELA Regents examination, which all students take in 11th grade. Task 3 of the ELA Regents exam requires that students read two passages of literature (usually a poem and either an essay or an excerpt) and then write a unified essay that develops a controlling idea shared by both passages. The students are also required to show how the authors use literary devices to develop the controlling idea. The following lesson, developed by South Side High School teacher Francesca Barberio, was designed with both of the above curricular goals in mind.

During the first semester of 10th grade, students read Mary Shelley's *Frankenstein*, William Golding's *Lord of the Flies*, and Shakespeare's *Macbeth*. Ms. Barberio chose a poem by Anne Sexton, *The Evil Seekers*, as the passage with which the students would compare these works, using the framework of the Regents Task 3. She chose the poem for both its rich imagery and its theme. Because evil and its emergence is an overarching theme of the three works previously read, the poem was an excellent match.

Ms. Barberio could have led a whole-class discussion to quickly analyze the poem. Instead, she chose to actively engage her students in the construction of their own analysis. She knew that some students would be struggle with a basic analysis of the poem, while other students were ready to be challenged to find deeper meaning. In the end, though, she needed to make sure that all students understood the poem, from the most basic to a more sophisticated level, in order to make the connections with the works that they had already read.

After a quick review of the requirements of a Task 3 essay, the class listened to the teacher read the poem, and then silently read it themselves. Each student received a handout with both the poem and three possible tasks, designated as Task A, Task B, and Task C. Ms. Barberio divided her 20 students into 5 heterogeneous groups and assigned each student Task A, B, or C to complete independently.

Students independently worked on the task they were assigned. Students who struggled with literary analysis were given Task A; the most proficient students were given Task C. The tasks were as follows:

Task A: Summarize the poem in your own words. What is the author saying to the reader? Circle all of the words in the poem that relate to good or evil. Identify the theme (message) of the poem.

Task B: Identify the theme of the poem. Annotate the literary devices that Anne Sexton uses to convey this theme. What effect do these devices have on the reader's understanding of this poem?

Task C: What is the author's message about human foibles? Notice the poet's use of pronouns in the text. How does the author skillfully use pronouns to move the reader from one section of the poem to the next? What is the effect of this shift? Imagine that this poem is a novel. Draw a line to separate one "chapter" from the next.

Students had a few minutes to complete their assigned task individually. Then they went to their numbered group to discuss their analysis. Each group was assigned one of the three works that they had studied. They were asked to discuss their responses to the task; find connections between the theme of the poem and their assigned work; identify a controlling idea connected to the themes of either evil or human foibles that was shared by both the poem and the work; and identify two literary devices or techniques from each text that best support that controlling idea.

Each member was assigned a role (e.g., text expert). All members had to be prepared to present their findings to the class. During presentations, students were required to take notes. For homework, they were allowed to choose one of the three novels and use their notes to write a Task 3 essay.

A 1st Grade Reading Lesson

First grade teacher Mary Hope Friedermann wanted to develop her students' listening, memory, and expressive skills. She could have read the class a story and then asked her students comprehension questions, resulting in one or two precocious students retelling the story. Instead, she chose to actively engage all students by using varied media based on the creativity and multiple intelligences of her students.

Ms. Friedermann began the class by reading aloud *The Umbrella* by Jan Brett. She then engaged the class in a brief book discussion to ensure that all could identify plot and character basics. Students helped the teacher create a class storyboard, using pictures and sentence strips to retell the story in sequential order.

It was then time for the students to retell the story on their own. Ms. Friedermann used students' multiple intelligences, interests, and strengths to assign them to appropriate groups. Each group of four students worked together to create a retelling of the story in one of the following ways:

• *Linguistic and intrapersonal.* Students complete a sequential retelling of *The Umbrella* using descriptive language to accurately retell the story in his/her own words.

• *Kinesthetic.* Using puppets and other props, students write, assign parts in, choreograph, and perform a skit to retell the story. Students are assisted by a teaching assistant for organizational purposes.

• *Spatial/visual.* Students use various arts and crafts supplies to create a group mural that identifies the story characters and retells the story through pictures.

• *Musical.* Students select words from a word bank to accurately complete a lyrical retelling of the story. Students perform the completed song accompanied by musical instruments.

• *Logical.* Students put sentence strips containing the events of the story in sequential order to complete an accurate retelling.

Ms. Friedermann assessed students' progress by observing them as they worked on their retelling projects. She also assessed their skill in working with others to achieve a common goal.

An 8th Grade Mathematics Lesson

It is often assumed that mathematics is the most difficult subject to detrack, and that differentiated instruction is not easily implemented in math classes. Coauthor Carol Corbett Burris decided to take on the challenge and design and teach the following beginning algebra lesson to our teachers during the staff development on differentiated instruction described in Chapter 5.

The objective of the lesson is for students to derive the slope intercept form of linear equations and then apply the equation to solve real-life problems. Carol began the lesson by telling a story about rising water in a pool. The story became a springboard to help participants ponder the concept of rate and realize that the height of the water is a dependent variable and that time is an independent variable.

The students (teachers and administrators) were divided into groups based on their academic department or area of expertise (e.g., elementary reading, mathematics). Each group solved the same problem; however, the presentation of their solutions varied in one of three ways. Some groups were to present their solution as a narrative explanation; others were to sketch a solution; and still others were to solve the problem using a graph. The problem and task descriptions can be found in Figure 6.2.

After the groups completed their tasks, Carol chose one person from each solution group to present to the class. She then taught a short mini-lesson that explored the concept of rate, and placed students in new groups. All but one of these groups was heterogeneous by achievement. The homogeneous "expert group" was composed of two to three students who were highly skilled in mathematics and could therefore take on extra challenge. Figure 6.3 shows the assigned problems.

FIGURE 6.2

Rising Water Problem and Differentiated Tasks

An empty, above-ground swimming pool is being filled with water. The water rises at a rate of 3 inches every 30 minutes. The pool is 6 feet deep. How much water will be in the pool after (a) 2.5 hours; (b) 3 hours; (c) 3.5 hours?

Task 1: Describe in a paragraph the relationship between time and the height of water, and then describe how you would solve the problem.

Task 2: Draw a representation of the problem that would lead to its solution. The pool should have a scale for height.

Task 3: Graph a solution to the problem with time on the x-axis and water height on the y-axis. Create a table of values for time (x) and height (y).

FIGURE 6.3

Additional Rising Water Problems

Each heterogeneous group was assigned one of the following problems:

1. An empty above-ground swimming pool is being filled with water. *The water now rises 15 inches every 45 minutes.* How much water will be in the pool after (a) 0.5 hours; (b) 2.5 hours; (c) 3.5 hours?

2. An empty above-ground swimming pool is being filled with water. There are two inches of water already in the pool. *The water rises at a rate of 4 inches every 30 minutes.* How much water will be in the pool after (a) 0.5 hours; (b) 2.5 hours; (c) 3.5 hours?

3. An empty above-ground swimming pool is being filled with water. Five inches of the pool is below ground level. *The water rises at a rate of 15 inches every 45 minutes.* What will be the height of the water in the pool *from ground level* after (a) 0.5 hours; (b) 2.5 hours; (c) 3.5 hours?

The "expert group" (composed of teachers with a strong background in mathematics) was given the three problems above along with the following instructions:

Read the three scenarios above. Create an equation that could be used to find solutions to all three problems, as well as the first problem solved by the class. The equation should be structured to solve for y, which represents height. Find solutions for all three scenarios using your equation.

These Instructions ask the expert group to derive the slope-intercept form ($y = mx + b$) of the linear equation, and then use it to solve the problems that the other groups were solving by graphing.

The teacher provided support as the groups worked on their problems. Groups that struggled were given scaffolding materials. After the problems were completed, the students reviewed the solutions. Using the overhead projector, a representative from each group showed their graph and explained the solution to their problem. Then the expert group explained the derivation of the equation and used that equation to find the solutions for the three problems. The whole class then used the equation to solve one additional problem.

Differentiated Lesson Design

Although each of the three sample lessons we've seen differs in content, they share common design principles based on the use of differentiated instruction in heterogeneous classes. First, each lesson was student-centered and constructivist. The teacher of the mathematics lesson could have given the equation of a line and had students do several practice problems. Instead, she allowed students to develop a deep understanding of the concept through graphing, verbal explanation, and sketching. The actual derivation of the equation was produced by the students and then practiced by all. Although talented students were given a special role, all students did meaningful work that contributed to the understanding of the entire class.

Second, even when tasks were tiered, all tasks made an important contribution to the lesson. This idea of meaningful work at different levels of proficiency is demonstrated well in the 10th grade English lesson. Even the most basic of the three tasks, the poem summary and identification of theme, was important work that was needed by the jigsaw group so that students could compare the poem with a previously read novel. The teacher carefully avoided using in-class tracking by having the students work on their initial tasks alone, and then asking them to share their work within their heterogeneous group. Teachers often use this model when differentiating by achievement to avoid creating groups of struggling students that are often off task. It also fosters a high level of individual accountability and active participation. The principles of the model are shown in Figure 6.4.

Third, the idea that students learn and express their knowledge through different modalities was included in each of the three lessons. In the first lesson, the teacher allowed learning to be socially constructed. In the second lesson, the teacher allowed students to retell the story in a variety of nontraditional ways. The third lesson used a narrative to begin a lesson in mathematics and integrated writing and artistic talents in solving the problems. None of the activities, however, was "fluff." Each brought students to the mastery of a clear and important learning objective.

FIGURE 6.4
_____

A Model for a Differentiated Lesson

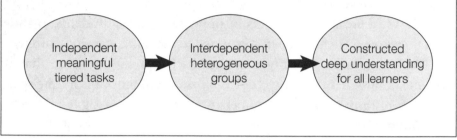

Although such lessons require extensive planning, if well-crafted, they are remarkably easy to teach. Most important, in differentiated cooperative lessons, learners are actively engaged throughout the lesson. The teacher is truly a "guide on the side" as students construct knowledge. We have seen this structure successfully used in all disciplines, from kindergarten through 12th grade, for both classroom activities and long-term projects.

Advice for Embedding Differentiated Practice

Helping a faculty learn to create constructivist, differentiated lessons is difficult. We have found that the lesson study model (Chokshi & Fernandez, 2005; Lewis, Perry, & Hurd, 2006) provides an excellent structure to have teachers develop and practice such lessons in a nonthreatening environment (see Chapter 5). Untenured teachers, and in some buildings tenured staff as well, teach a differentiated lesson as one of their formally observed lessons. Weekly lesson plans are carefully read, and suggestions for differentiation are provided as feedback.

As teachers examine lessons for differentiation, the following questions can foster discussion:

1. Are all students engaged throughout the lesson? Are reluctant learners given a voice? Are they held responsible for their classwork?

2. Does the teacher use multiple modalities to present information?

3. Are questions and problems tiered in a meaningful manner, allowing all students to contribute to the discussion? Is there sufficient wait time after each question? Are questions asked on a variety of levels (e.g., Bloom's taxonomy)?

4. Are there different kinds of opportunities for students to show what they know? Are all students expected to meet the learning objective?

5. Is the lesson well organized, with clear instructions, so that all students know what they are to do? Is a minimum amount of time spent on organization? Are group membership and/or tasks assigned thoughtfully and quickly?

We refer you again to Appendix B, which contains a rubric for differentiated instruction. It can serve as a helpful guide for self-reflection for teachers who are integrating differentiated techniques into their lessons.

Varied Learning Assessments

We are acutely aware of the mandates of the No Child Left Behind act. While we are dismayed by the overwhelming number of examinations that even young students must take, we agree that it is the obligation of schools to help all students meet high learning standards. Therefore, although we suggest differentiating *the ways* in which we assess student learning, we are not suggesting creating "easier" assessments for some students. Instead, use a variety of ways to document and measure student learning.

In detracked classes, students' learning should be assessed in ways that recognize their differing levels of prior achievement and their uniqueness as individual learners. For example, at the elementary level we have put in place districtwide mandated math assessments for each unit of study to ensure that all middle school students can successfully complete algebra by the end of 8th grade. These teacher-designed parallel assessments include five questions modeled after the state exam format. The assessments are cumulative in nature and are administered bimonthly. Within each unit of study, teachers design spiral activities to reinforce or enrich concepts and skills based on individual students' needs as demonstrated in the assessments. Based on these spiral reviews, teachers reinforce or enrich topics. Each teacher has a binder of spiral activities that are based on prior units of study and coded by skill and concept. Often teachers use "Problem of the Day" activities that are differentiated based on the previously mentioned assessment tools to achieve the same goal of reinforcement or enrichment.

Eighth-grade ELA teachers include choice of product in their final assessment for their nonfiction unit. These assessments, which are based on the oral commentary requirements of the IB, acknowledge the multiple intelligences of their students. Using the course anthology, students read a variety of nonfiction texts related to the theme of preserving memory. These texts include a biographical essay, a persuasive essay, and poetry. Throughout the unit, teachers emphasize the active reading strategy of visualization, encouraging students to search for descriptive language to make pictures in their minds, sketch the scene in their journals, and add details to the picture as they continued to read. Students may choose to apply visualization in their oral presentation as their final assessment. The requirements of the culminating activity are included in Figure 6.5.

For each of the readings, the students use a graphic organizer to record the title, genre, and author's purpose, along with text support and the nonfiction structure (i.e., sequence, cause/effect, compare/contrast, problem/solution, description). As each student or pair of students presents their project, the other students use a sticky note to comment on the presentation with these questions as a guide: How did I feel? What did I see? What did I think? What did I hear? What was the author's purpose? These same questions were used throughout the unit when the students had to determine the author's purpose.

In the high schools, the rich learning assessments of the IB program influence assignments in grades 9–12. For example, in addition to the formal external assessment at the end of the English IB course, students are required to write a world literature paper over the course of two years, to make a formal oral commentary on a literary passage to the class, and

FIGURE 6.5

8th Grade Oral Presentation Guidelines

During our nonfiction unit, we have read a plethora of pieces that piqued our interest in many areas. As a culmination to this unit, you will be asked to revisit one of the selections we have read and make an oral presentation to the class. Your presentation must show a deep understanding of the text. You may work with a partner with teacher's approval. You may select from *one* of the following activities:

1. "The Story of Maya Ying Lin" discussed the creation of the Vietnam Memorial.
   a. Write and deliver the commencement address that Maya might have given at her high school describing her thoughts about setting goals and inspiring the students to achieve their dreams.
   b. Dramatically read the section of the story that describes the goals/criteria/requirements of the Vietnam Memorial Contest as designed by the Vietnam Veterans' Memorial Fund.
   c. Create a memorial of your choice and compare this to Maya Ying Lin's.

2. "The Story of Your Life" or "Wahbegan."
   a. Dramatically read or memorize one of the above poems.
   b. Create a memorial of your choice, and compare this to "The Story of Your Life" or "Wahbegan."

3. "Baseball" describes a unique brand of baseball.
   a. Dramatically read the rules of the game so that one might be able to play the game.
   b. Create a visual to represent either this game or a game of your choice showing the rules of the game. If it is your own choice, show your game's connection to "Baseball."

4. "Debbie" or "Forest Fire" or "How to Be Polite Online."
   a. Dramatically read your selection as a radio address.
   b. Create and read a children's picture book depicting the essence of the story "Debbie."
   c. Using the descriptive language in the story "Forest Fire," create a visual representing parts of the text.
   d. Using "How to Be Polite Online," update the rules of Internet use; create a chart to use with your presentation.

FIGURE 6.5

8th Grade Oral Presentation Guidelines (*continued*)

5. "Saving the Wetlands" is a persuasive essay that deals with a young boy's concern with the wetlands in his hometown.

   a. On page 279, Andy Holleman speaks at a town meeting expressing his concerns about the wetlands. He begins by saying, "You call yourself the Russell Mill Pond Realty Trust, Inc." Although he continues briefly, the author does not include his full speech. In this presentation, you are to write what you believe would be his full speech and deliver it to the "town board" (class). Your goal is to convince us of your concerns for the wetlands and what you believe would be the results if the condominiums were to be built.

   b. Design a real estate advertisement for the condominiums that would have been developed on the wetlands. Use evidence from the text.

6. "Hokusai: The Old Man Mad About Drawing" is a biographical essay about a man who introduced innovative art forms throughout his life.

   a. In this presentation you will select from the media that Hokusai worked in (or one of your own) and demonstrate to your audience how to create the piece.

   b. Memorize and present Hokusai's description of his life on page 655.

7. (With prior teacher approval) design your own presentation based on a reading in the anthology.

Source: Ronnie Dien, Jeanne Radigan, Marie Fircz, and Mary T. Fletcher, South Side Middle School, Rockville Centre, New York.

to engage in one-on-one commentary with the teacher, which is taped for possible external evaluation.

Beginning in 9th grade, South Side High School students regularly make oral presentations. Writing is a serious academic endeavor. Writing portfolios in both English and social studies measure student growth, promote reflection, and reward progress. The process and product rubrics described in Chapter 2 assess effort as well as growth in learning outcomes. Students participate both individually and cooperatively in historical investigations and debates. They create math "investigations" in pre-calculus classes, and detailed lab reports are an integral part of science education. Although each student takes the same assessments, such a variety of assessments allows teachers to honor students' multiple intelligences. All assessments, however, reflect rigorous learning standards and are intended to prepare students for success on both New York State Regents examinations and IB assessments.

Ways to Meet the Needs of All Learners

Schools have an obligation to meet the needs of all learners, and in a detracked school that obligation must be met in thoughtful and individualized ways. There are no low-track classes in which to hide underperforming students. Likewise, there are no gates to the high-track curriculum to close out students who are less motivated or have weaker academic preparation. Gifted students are not isolated from their peers, so their teachers must provide the appropriate challenge to meet their needs within the context of the curriculum. Finally, students with learning disabilities are included in the rich curriculum rather than assigned to self-contained classrooms where they work on skills throughout the day. Support systems both within and outside of their classrooms must help them compensate for their disability. In short, in detracked schools, students must receive personalized learning experiences that will allow them to succeed and thrive in a community that includes all learners (Garrity & Burris, 2007).

Support Systems for Leveled-Up Classes

Our elementary schools employ a team approach to support students in a rich, challenging elementary instructional program. The team consists of the classroom teacher and ESL, special education, math, and ELA support teachers as needed. Based on the performance of each incoming kindergarten student on the DIAL (Developmental Indicators for the Assessment of Learning) and ESI (Early Screening Inventory), the team determines individualized support services from the beginning of the student's educational experience. The classroom teacher identifies other students in need of assistance as they progress through their K–5 experience.

We use a six-day cycle for all support programs based on a push-in model, whereby members of the support team are scheduled to take part in the regular elementary classrooms. ELA instruction is mandated for 90 minutes daily. Guided reading is the most common support offered by the team. For 45 minutes every other day, or three days in the six-day cycle, a team composed of the ELA support teacher, teaching assistants, and one or more of the other support staff (e.g., ESL, special ed) push into the regular classroom to provide small-group instruction based on students' progress in reading. The groups are fluid in that students move among groups based on the team's recommendation, and the teachers and teaching assistants rotate among the groups as well. Additionally, some students may be seen in a small group or individually for the remaining 45 minutes for more intensive intervention.

The district mandates one hour of daily mathematics instruction in grades K–5. The math support teacher pushes in to the regular classrooms twice in the six-day cycle in grades 3–5 and once in the six-day cycle for grades K–2. The math-support service varies depending upon the needs of the students and the class as a whole. The support teacher may work with a small group, an individual, or the entire class (to allow the classroom teacher to target students).

Planning is a critical part of the success of the elementary program. The teachers' contract includes 30 minutes daily before school for professional meetings. Once in a six-day cycle, the teachers join with the support team by grade level to plan instruction, discuss individual students, or meet with parents. The schedule generally follows the model shown in Figure 6.6. Blank slots allow for extra help, parent conferences, and teacher planning.

In the middle and high schools, support classes allow teachers to pre- and post-teach curriculum to small groups of students. The key to support-class success is that it is not remedial in nature, but rather supports the curriculum (Oakes, 2005). For example, prior to the introduction of a new topic in mathematics, students may practice using the graphing calculator in their support class so that they will be ready to participate when the calculator is used during the topic. In an ELA support class, students may do a group reading of the text with the teacher,

FIGURE 6.6

Planning Cycle for the Elementary Support Teams

Day	K	1	2	3	4	5
1	Math			STELLAR	Grade level	ELA
2	ELA	Math			STELLAR	Grade level
3	Grade level	ELA	Math			STELLAR
4	STELLAR	Grade level	ELA	Math		
5		STELLAR	Grade level	ELA	Math	
6			STELLAR	Grade level	ELA	Math

annotating, highlighting, and completing a graphic organizer on character or plot. In science-support classes, students might receive assistance in writing up a difficult laboratory report or watch a video clip of the circulatory system to help reinforce content. By keeping support classes small (12 students or fewer), teachers can provide the individualized attention students need to succeed.

There are other ways to provide support when all students take a challenging curriculum. In the high school, a teaching assistant is available in the library to provide homework assistance after school. In the middle school, the district funds The Learning Center (TLC) for 40 minutes after school for homework assistance. TLC is by invitation only in order to target specific students. Group membership changes based on students' needs. In addition, by negotiated contract, middle and high school teachers provide extra help for one half-hour prior to the start of school four out of five mornings a week. Many high school teachers forgo study hall or hall duty to staff a resource center during their duty period. They provide help for any student who has a free period and comes to the center looking for academic assistance. By reallocating staffing, working with the teachers' association to modify the contract, and using paraprofessionals in creative ways, schools can provide opportunities to support students learning a challenging curriculum.

The programs that we have discussed are just a sample of the many that detracking schools have put in place to support students in taking rigorous curriculum. Summer preparation programs and weekend programs are used by schools to accelerate learning and provide academic counseling. National programs such as AVID (Nelson, 2007) have had great success in providing the additional support that students need to take college preparatory courses.

Challenge for the High Achiever

The research on the effects of tracking on the performance of high achievers has been mixed. Some argue that the elimination of tracking will result in reducing the achievement of a school's most talented and motivated students (Brewer, Rees, & Argys, 1995; Loveless, 1999). Our studies (Burris et al., 2006; Burris et al., 2007) as well as the studies of others (Mosteller, Light, & Sachs, 1996; Slavin, 1990) have found that the achievement of highly talented students either is not affected or actually increases when detracking occurs. The key factor, of course, is ensuring that the curriculum remains challenging.

In addition to teaching the former high-track curriculum to detracked classes, schools can provide opportunities for high-achieving students who require additional challenge. For example, at both the middle and high school levels, our district offers elective courses in both the arts and science research to promote the creative expression of talent. In the 10th grade, there is a supplemental elective in chemistry and mathematics for students who wish to go beyond the standard curriculum. In keeping with district philosophy, these courses are open to any student who wishes to take them in addition to the basic, heterogeneous course. Extracurricular activities, especially those that involve interschool academic competitions, can provide additional intellectual stimulation.

In the elementary schools, each classroom teacher team teaches with the STELLAR teacher once in the six-day cycle to enrich the grade-level curriculum. The STELLAR teacher combines the roles of technology teacher, enrichment/gifted teacher, and library media specialist. The program uses Renzulli's schoolwide enrichment model (Renzulli, 1994; Renzulli & Reis,

1997), which includes Type I general exploratory activities that expose children to an array of experiences beyond the classroom via visiting authors and artists; Type II group activities that include development of critical thinking skills, research skills, and written, oral, and visual communication skills; and Type III individual and small-group experiences that provide opportunities for advanced study and research in areas of interest. Following Renzulli's philosophy that "a rising tide lifts all ships," we offer the three types of enrichment to all students, believing that enrichment, not remediation, will develop the talents of each student (Renzulli & Reis, 1997). Figure 6.7 gives examples of enrichment projects used in our elementary schools.

Grade-level groups of teachers collaborate with the building STELLAR teacher to select a curriculum topic, design correlating enrichment activities, and identify students for further enrichment on the topic. Above and beyond the single STELLAR period, the STELLAR teacher offers small-group and individual extension activities based on student interest. STELLAR activities may take other forms depending upon the needs (and creativity) of the students, the teaching staff, the building, or the district at large.

Some buildings determine an enrichment theme for the year, for example, a science research project in which each grade level, K–5, selects a curriculum topic, and each student or small groups of students conduct in-depth research on a segment of the topic that interests them. A Family Science Fair then celebrates the enrichment activities with a visual display and oral presentation by each group.

Each year, the STELLAR and 5th grade teachers participate in a Type III activity known as the JASON Project (www.jason.org), an expedition-based multimedia science education program sponsored by National Geographic. One year, this project included the study of monster storms and wetlands via online communication and collaboration with scientists in the field. Through the JASON Project, students choose from a variety of topics, activities, and experiments, discovering "real science in real time." Some 5th graders researched the ecosystems of the wetlands, completed a local aquatic field study, and uploaded data to JASON scientists, while

FIGURE 6.7
_____

Applications of Schoolwide Enrichment in the STELLAR Program

Type I Enrichment: Sparking Interest

- *Literacy Week:* Participate in a celebration of reading and writing that includes visiting authors and poets.

- *Project Wilderness:* Engage in online communication with scientists exploring the Amazon.

- *Enrichment Clusters:* Attend self-selected workshops offered by staff members to learn about a topic.

Type II Enrichment: Developing Affective and Cognitive Skills

- *Kindergarten:* Develop affective behaviors of respect and cognitive skills of observation and communication through a hands-on "Egg to Chick" unit.

- *Grade 1:* Develop oral communication skills and creativity through a dramatic retelling of a folktale.

- *Grade 4:* Develop advanced research skills, values clarification, and communication skills through a debate on the pros and cons of the whaling industry in New England in the 1850s.

Type III Enrichment: Synthesis and Application

- *Pursuing Passions K–5:* Conduct in-depth research on a self-selected topic.

- *JASON Project, Grade 5:* Participate in this National Geographic program linked to scientists in the field.

- *Grades 4–5:* Analyze number puzzles and create a how-to manual with sample puzzles. Research, design, and create a school mural as an extension of a curriculum topic.

others created artistic renderings of the wetlands. Students expanded their understanding of hurricanes using a virtual hurricane-tracking device and applied that knowledge to identifying potential hazards on Long Island. They used a global positioning system to observe the effects of weather and environmental conditions. All students collaborated with their peers, increased their knowledge of science, and applied that knowledge in a self-selected area of study.

Beyond such "extras," however, teachers have an obligation to differentiate instruction in all classes to meet the needs of students who excel as well as those who are challenged. The following are some examples of such differentiation:

- The incorporation of questions that require students to analyze, synthesize, and evaluate information
- Differentiated projects and homework assignments that cater to student interest and choice
- Books at a variety of reading levels in elementary and middle school classes
- The assignment or option of more challenging readings at the high school level
- Extension activities that allow students to further their understanding or explore an interest
- Differentiated homework problems at a higher level of challenge in math and science classes

Our teachers are constantly examining, learning, practicing, and refining new strategies that mesh with their teaching style and the needs of the learners that they serve. There are many excellent books that provide examples of sophisticated strategies for differentiating instruction. We highly recommend the work of Carol Ann Tomlinson. Her ASCD book *How to Differentiate Instruction in Mixed-Ability Classrooms* (2001) is a wonderful primer and introduction to the topic. This book, along with her more recent works, provides an excellent description of techniques that include curriculum compacting, concept-based teaching, learning contracts, and other innovative strategies.

Special Education Services

In a school committed to excellence and equity, all schooling routines that result in the separation of students from each other need to be reinvented and reconfigured. The traditional approach of providing instruction to students with learning disabilities in a separate setting is not in concert with the beliefs of a school in which all students are part of the learning community and welcomed into all classes. Although students with special needs may require targeted services, pullout programs should become push-in programs whenever possible (Ascher, 1992).

All learners in grades K–5, including those who are developmentally delayed, such as students with Down syndrome, are included in our district's elementary school classes. Beginning in 6th grade, developmentally delayed students take separate academic and life-skills programs in the middle and high schools, as well as mainstream elective courses. All other special education students are included in the mainstream program in grades K–12 through the practice of inclusion.

Our elementary special education teachers assigned to inclusion students push into classrooms for a minimum of one period per day; secondary special education teachers push into classes every other day. A full-time teaching assistant is assigned to each classroom with inclusion students to provide support when the special education teacher is not there. All teachers, elementary and secondary, are expected to ensure that special education teachers and assistants have an active role in instruction that is included in their lesson plans.

In addition to the support services described above, special education students in grades 6–12 meet with a special education teacher who is a specialist both in the content area and in teaching compensatory learning strategies. During this time (usually one instructional period each day), special education teachers help students meet the goals on their individualized education plans, using the curriculum as the medium. The goal of the program is to teach students the strategies that will help compensate for their disability, thus helping them to become independent learners in the world of work or higher education.

A Teacher's Voice on Differentiation

As we stated at the beginning of this chapter, helping a faculty progress from traditional lessons to differentiated, student-centered lessons is a difficult process that requires thought, creativity, and patience. It seems only fitting, then, that we should conclude this chapter with the voice of high school English teacher Christine Brown, a master teacher who not only uses differentiated instruction in her classroom but helped design and teach courses on differentiation to her colleagues.

As an English teacher, I am always searching for the perfect metaphor to simplify a challenging concept. For me, differentiated instruction is best related to the game of baseball. As the pitcher of concepts and ideas, the teacher must be sure that not every pitch comes across the plate in the very same way. Variety keeps the game interesting for everyone. As the batter, a student will be most engaged in the game if he or she comes to bat not knowing what to expect. Students should have experience with several different pitches, but not know which one will be used on any given day. To conclude the extended metaphor, one must remember that the game of baseball is a team sport, whereby each player takes a different position based on his or her skill set. All positions are important and necessary to win the game!

Consider the following tools for building a differentiated learning environment for your students:

– *Choice.* Give students a say in how they learn and demonstrate understanding. Decision making is an important skill that can be taught in a differentiated instruction model. A simple way to offer choice is to offer students a homework menu. Allow them to be part of the process by choosing the best way to show what they know. Homework responses will be differentiated and make a great fodder for sharing with peers on the day they are due.

– *Learning how to learn.* Rather than focus instruction entirely on *what* we learn, consider letting the students in on "the big secret" regarding *how* we learn. Teaching should be transparent for the learner.

– *Routine.* Develop consistent classroom routines to facilitate smooth transitions between activities.

– *Understanding the whole student.* Get to know your students well—not only their achievement, but their talents and intelligences. An interest inventory and multiple intelligences assessment are two excellent activities for the beginning of the school year.

– *Varied assessments.* There is more than one way for students to show what they know!

– *Varied materials.* Use several elements and materials to support instructional content.

– *Collegiality.* Teachers are learners. They must support each other through the process of trying something new. Similarly, students should support each other in the classroom. Community building is key!

– *Student talk.* Give students an opportunity to share ideas and engage in rich discussion. Allow enough time for learners to become engaged and involved in the subject. Remember, the students must remain active and responsible explorers.

– *Connection.* Personal connections and bridging information are both important in the effort to make meaning.

– *Appropriate repetition of a lesson structure.* In class, repetition of a strategy is important in order for students to master necessary skills and become comfortable with a particular style of lesson. For example, it may take several jigsaw lessons before students are able to work efficiently in the model.

– *Learning modalities.* Students learn in a variety of ways. Teachers should provide opportunities to acquire knowledge and skills through a variety of experiences. Do not try to incorporate all learning modalities in each lesson. Rather, choose those that best fit the content. Students should be encouraged to share their talents as well as try something new.

– *The rule of odd numbers.* It is recommended that students be given an unusual or odd number of minutes in which to complete a task (e.g., 4 minutes instead of 5 minutes). This will raise their level of concern for completing the task and keep them focused on timing.

– *Flexible grouping.* Students should be given the opportunity to work with the same group more than once to build trust and efficiency among members, if the group works well together. Student groups should be periodically changed to provide opportunity for new collaborative relationships.

– *Balance.* Provide a balance between teacher-assigned and student-selected tasks.

– *Multicultural appreciation.* Powerful differences exist among the students in a class. Afford opportunities to celebrate culture and experience.

– *Different teaching styles.* Teachers who differentiate instruction must never stop reinventing themselves. The pedagogical "bag of tricks" can always be stuffed with a few new ideas. This is what makes teaching an ever-changing art form.

Teachers like Christine Brown are natural leaders. They love their craft and constantly reflect upon their practice. They are the teachers from whom school leaders learn. Not every teacher, however, internalizes staff development quickly. Some are willing, but they struggle with new practices. And some are resistant, either actively or passively, to any new reform in their school. They hunker down and wait for the "new wave" of staff development to pass.

Without care and constant support, reforms, especially detracking reforms, will quickly unravel. It is easy for teachers to slip back into old practices and old expectations about who can learn and what they should be learning. And it is always easy to find parents who would like tracking to return. Alliances between unhappy teachers and parents can quickly form and undermine progress. Thus, the most difficult aspect of any school reform is maintaining the change in practice, embedding it in school culture, and moving it forward. In the next chapter, we share some strategies that can be used to increase the probability for both long- and short-term success.

7

Maintaining the Reform and Pushing Forward

Rockville Centre School District's detracking reform began in 1986. After more than 20 years, one might think that our staff would be on automatic pilot, but that is not the case. As with any systemic reform, detracking requires day-to-day leadership and vigilance. We find ourselves continually reaffirming our philosophy to constituent groups, listening to the shouts and the whispers, selecting and mentoring new staff, carefully supervising instruction, and collaborating with all constituencies.

Presenting a United Front

Learning how to establish and maintain a united front in the face of criticism is critical when you are engaged in a school reform such as detracking. The key is open and informed communication. Board of Education members are the front-line recipients of issues and complaints from stakeholders at their homes, in the community, and at public meetings. Each trustee must be well informed and well educated, from the initial discussions regarding leveling up a course curriculum to the changes in teacher practices that occur as a result of detracking. Our district's superintendent communicates with the trustees in writing three times each week. He includes professional articles that provide background knowledge and

research regarding an existing or proposed program, curriculum development proposals, and descriptions of instructional strategies. For example,
when the district pursued initiatives in reading and writing in the content
areas, he shared an article on the use of poetry to build literacy in content
areas. During a public review of the budget, a community member challenged a curriculum project titled "Poetry in Science K–5." The board
members, along with the assistant superintendent for curriculum and
instruction, were able to articulate the research on the use of poetry in
science to develop vocabulary in a different genre. They explained how
poetry might enable students to make personal connections to topics,
thus developing a deeper understanding of the science content (Kane &
Rule, 2004).

The Board of Education requests presentations of quantitative and
qualitative data showing year-to-year and longitudinal growth. These presentations are often linked to professional development initiatives and
curricular changes. They inform the public about the critical roles that
teacher education and curriculum upgrading play in the success of our
students in heterogeneous classes.

Although we strongly suggest that you always present quantitative
achievement data as you detrack, qualitative data, such as student work,
can also help the public understand how learning is improving as a result
of the reform. For example, during the focus on reading and writing in the
content areas, two representatives of each building design team from the
elementary, middle, and high schools presented the different purposes for
writing: to explore, expand, inform, revise, entertain, reflect, evaluate, analyze, or persuade. Each team addressed one of the purposes using authentic student writing. The teachers displayed both fiction and nonfiction
pieces of student work, described the instructional plan that yielded the
piece, and highlighted the means of differentiating the writing instruction.
Teachers carefully explained and demonstrated how they meet the needs
of individual students through the use of models, purposeful brainstorm-
ing, transitional words and phrases, writing prompts, graphic organizers,
inspirational readings, and student research. Teachers also described specific tips for parents to incorporate writing in daily activities. The parents

received a packet that was concurrently posted on the district Web site as a reference.

Building and central office administrators must also be well informed and well educated regarding all facets of a systemic reform. Monthly district administrative team meetings provide a forum for proposing, discussing, and planning instructional change. Administrators participate in all professional development initiatives as facilitator or participant. Central office administrators present the rationale for initiatives as well as the budget implications, the implementation model, and the evaluation plan in districtwide forums. They regularly review disaggregated quantitative data from the required No Child Left Behind (NCLB) assessments. They carefully review the data in the aggregate and by demographic groups, including special education, minority, and low socioeconomic status students. Longitudinal studies provide comparative data for student performance as the district expands detracking across grade levels and subject areas.

Building administrators must be well prepared to address issues and concerns from parents and teachers. They should report assessment data at faculty and PTA meetings to publicly share their building's success and to acknowledge those areas where improvement is still needed. Parents typically speak with teachers before they speak with administrators about their child's progress in a course, and often share their feelings about the course and curriculum. Therefore, teachers must be well informed and know that they are supported by the building administration when they are challenged by a parent who does not necessarily believe in detracking. From initial discussions to staff and curriculum development, teachers are active participants in the continuum of the reform process. Building administrators nurture the culture through thoughtful dialog at grade-level meetings at the elementary level and departmental meetings at the secondary level. Joining administrative and teacher forces through open discussions and opportunities for shared leadership solidifies the instructional team.

Community members need a full understanding of the process and goals of detracking in order to support and maintain the reform. Parents can be strong allies in initiating, maintaining, and expanding detracking. It is important that teachers and administrators be good listeners and hear what is stated, implied, or not stated, both aloud and in whispers. The importance of taking the pulse of parents cannot be overestimated, as they have the potential to organize, for better or for worse, around an issue and either effect or stonewall change. Parents were not taught in heterogeneous classrooms using differentiated instruction, and much of what you discuss may be new to them.

Beyond PTA meetings and Board of Education meetings, our district established other forums for parents to receive information and voice their opinions regarding the change process. The district's instructional and achievement goals and the data to support them are common talking points in each of the following groups:

• *PTA Curriculum Committee.* A teacher and a parent from each of the district's seven schools, including a parent and teacher from special education, participate in the Parent-Teacher Association (PTA) Curriculum Committee. The group meets monthly with the assistant superintendent for instruction to address curriculum concerns. The representatives share information regarding curriculum initiatives with the local PTA and school faculty and bring curriculum concerns from the local group to the district committee. This joint committee of teachers, parents, and administrators has proven to be a dynamic forum for in-depth discussions regarding questions and concerns about detracking.

• *PTA Presidents.* The superintendent meets monthly with the presidents of each building's PTA and SEPTA (Special Education PTA). The agenda includes items from all members. The superintendent uses this forum to test the waters by initially introducing an educational change that has been discussed and recommended by the principals. He also reviews data from external assessments and receives feedback on hot topics of discussion at the local level. The co-chairs of this group also meet separately with the superintendent as needed to keep lines of communication open between parents and administration.

• *PTA Council.* A member of the Board of Education meets monthly with this council composed of members of the executive board of each PTA. The council discusses changes in instruction, budgetary issues, and general parental concerns. When requested, a member of the central office administration attends the meeting.

• *SEPTA.* SEPTA is a PTA organization composed of parents and teachers of special education students and central office special education staff. The group meets monthly and usually has a guest speaker on a topic of interest to the group. As self-contained special education classes were dismantled, discussions with this group were critical to building confidence in the model, developing an understanding of the goals, and sharing pre- and post-implementation achievement data.

• *Building Site-Based Team.* Students, parents, teachers, and administrators participate in this building-based group. Here again, each member represents a constituency group with whom they share information and from whom they receive questions to be presented at future meetings.

Working with Doubting Teachers

As we have discussed throughout this book, not all members of the teaching staff initially supported the district's philosophy of offering all students the opportunity to study a rigorous curriculum in heterogeneous classes. Even today, some struggle with reconciling the ideal of equity with their beliefs about human intelligence.

Teachers also feel threatened when they are asked to change their tried-and-true instructional methodologies. Some enjoyed their status as the "honors" teacher, as discussed in Chapter 4. Whenever our district introduced a new detracked curriculum, there were doubters. From time to time, we needed to hold frequent meetings to closely monitor the new curriculum's implementation in order to ensure not just the correct level of difficulty and complexity of instruction but also the effective implementation of support classes. Teachers need to know that they are supported in their work and that school leaders are listening. They must have confidence that administrators will do their best to remove any roadblocks that impede their students' success.

We have had some instances of teachers trying to enlist the support of parents to undermine the implementation of the detracking program. In these cases, administrators met directly with the staff members to discuss the situation, listen to their concerns, offer any assistance short of changing the program, and in some cases, ask the person to suspend their disbelief until the model had been fully implemented for the year. The teachers were assured that if the data did not result in growth and success for the students, modifications and adjustments would be made. It is understood, however, that returning to tracked classes is not an acceptable modification.

Working with Doubting Parents

Keeping parents fully informed about the reform in general, and about their child's progress in the program specifically, are essential. Our schools have formal committees and forums in place to assist parents in developing a deep understanding of goals and comprehending the changes that are needed to achieve the goals. This kind of outreach must be supplemented with personalized communication with those parents who voice concerns. Teachers, guidance counselors, and administrators must keep the lines of communication open.

One evening there was a heated discussion at a PTA Curriculum Committee meeting on whether detracking made sense for struggling students. Some parent members voiced their concern that detracking was not good for all children's self-esteem. The assistant superintendent reviewed the data on the success of the initiative for all students and showed the substantial growth each year for students who in the past would have been relegated to self-contained or low-track classes. Although in the end not all parents agreed, the majority came to appreciate how detracking provides students with opportunities that they would not have had prior to the reform and how, even if lower achievers struggled, heterogeneous classes were a far better alternative than low-track classes with fewer learning opportunities.

Setting New Goals and Seizing Opportunities for Change

In conjunction with the central office administration, building teams analyze the data from all external assessments and monitor participation and student success. We affirm and celebrate the success of our schools by sharing this information in the many forums named above, as well as by publishing data in school and district newsletters and local newspapers. Based on the data, the superintendent and Board of Education determine new achievement goals for the district and set instructional goals for continued reform.

Outside mandates, however, can also serve as catalysts for change and provide the leverage needed to implement detracking. NCLB requires assessments of students in grades 3 through 8 in ELA and mathematics, and as an ancillary requirement mandates academic support for any student, including those receiving special education, who does not reach proficiency. This requirement reinforces the delivery of supplementary instruction in support classes to students who struggle. Further, these mandates help the public understand that increased levels of spending are necessary to meet NCLB standards.

When New York State revises the curriculum, it provides an opportunity to institute detracking. For example, the detracking of our 9th grade science course coincided with the shift from the old New York State course in biology to the new course titled The Living Environment. There have also been tipping points where large numbers of students chose to "level up" to a higher-level course, leaving very few students in a lower-track class. Detracking was able to proceed smoothly by moving all students to the highest instructional level. Teachers of the lower-track class have typically become the initiators of this change after having seen the dramatic difference in academic tone, depth of discussions, and academic role models in the two levels of a course. Based on the ongoing analysis of data, the time for change presents itself. Discussions with departmental staff, district administrators, the Board of Education, and parents begin. The process always requires a thorough review of the trends in the present data, review of past success in other subjects, and a detailed implementation plan including staffing, curriculum writing, and professional training.

Selecting Staff

When hiring new teachers, it is important to ascertain whether their philosophy and beliefs are a good fit for a detracked school (Welner & Oakes, 2000). One place to begin is by asking a candidate to describe his or her teaching experience with varying levels of a course (e.g., Honors English 7, Regular English 7, and Skills English 7). Often applicants will list accomplishments, such as "designed activities for gifted students" and "created test prep materials for lower-ability students." During the interview, you can follow up with questions that will encourage the candidate to speak about his or her philosophy and beliefs. Such questions might include the following:

1. "Describe a lesson that you taught in your honors class. How would this differ from a lesson in your regular class?"

2. "Do you think any of your regular students could succeed in an honors level class? Why or why not?"

3. "Describe an activity that you created for your gifted students. If you were teaching a class that was heterogeneous, could you incorporate that activity? How?"

4. "What strategies do you employ with your special education students?"

Questions that allow prospective administrators to speak about their philosophy and beliefs include the following:

1. "What are the criteria for students to be selected for the honors program in your present school?"

2. "What is your opinion of the criteria?"

3. "Can a student move up to an honors level? What do you think of such movement?"

4. "Describe the difference between the honors and regular curricula."

5. "What do you say to parents who want their child in honors courses for which the child doesn't meet the criteria? How do you feel during such conversations?"

There are educators who would be successful in a tracked school but would not succeed in a detracked, inclusive environment. Teachers don't necessarily have to have experience in teaching detracked classes to be successful, but they must have an open mind and a willingness to adjust their instructional repertoire. Administrators must express a comfort level and deep belief in offering all students an equitable, high-quality education. If they have any doubt about the philosophy of an inclusive program with no gates to the best courses of study, they will project their skepticism to teachers, students, and parents.

Supervising Instruction

For all students, the quality of the instruction they receive makes a difference. Researchers have long established that there are observable differences in the classroom instruction provided by effective and ineffective schools, and that the principal plays a critical role in supporting quality instruction (Teddlie, Kirby, & Stringfield, 1989). As finding highly skilled teachers becomes increasingly more difficult, especially for inner-city schools, it is essential that all teachers be given the guidance and support that will allow them to be the most effective teachers that they can be. That requires that school leaders immerse themselves in curriculum and instruction.

In detracked schools, instructional leadership is vital to ensuring that instructional goals are rigorous and on an honors level, and that teachers are not "teaching to the middle." Likewise, instructional leaders must guide and support teachers to ensure that instruction is being differentiated and that all learners' voices are heard in the classroom. Teachers must work together so that support classes are aligned with the course curriculum. And finally, there should be feedback and supportive coaching so that teachers can adjust their instruction to help all learners be successful.

Becoming familiar with curriculum, reviewing lesson plans and student work, and of course, observing and coaching teachers are all important components of good instructional leadership. If new instructional strategies are needed as a school opens access to excellence, changing practices should be planned and observable. It is easy for critics to throw up their hands and say that detracking is impossible. It is the principal and assistant administrators who must provide the day-to-day vigilance necessary for successful reform.

We have found the following strategies to be effective in helping school leaders provide support for teachers as they adjust during the transition from tracked to detracked classes.

The Importance of the Lesson Plans

More than 20 years ago, one of us heard instructional guru Madeline Hunter say that it takes four times as long to plan an excellent lesson as it does to teach it. Although it is impossible for teachers to spend that amount of time planning every lesson, Hunter's underlying message—that planning is critical for good instruction—is as true now as it was then. Indeed, the practice of lesson study is founded on the belief that the planning of a lesson is so important that input from colleagues is essential for the creation of an expert lesson. Such collaborative lesson development not only results in a cache of expert lessons, it also helps teachers develop new pedagogical strategies that can be transferred to other lessons. In short, the planning of a lesson is as important as its execution, and it makes sense for school leaders to pay attention to the planning process. It is also important that principals and other school leaders who are undergoing detracking reform take the time to read and review plans to make sure that instruction is changing as classes become more heterogeneous and new curriculum is taught.

The first thing to look for in any lesson, be it traditional or constructivist, is a well-articulated objective that is linked to goals of the curriculum. Often beginning teachers (and sometimes veterans) look for clever and engaging activities for their classes, with only a vague notion of how the activities support learning. If learning standards are to remain high and connected to curricular goals, it is critical that the objective comes first, with all activities designed to support it.

Lesson plans should also communicate how differentiation is incorporated and the role of support staff in the lesson. Both will occur only if they are planned events. Figure 7.1 describes what to look for when reviewing plans for detracked classes.

One effective way to review lesson plans is to use e-mail. Coauthor and principal Carol Corbett Burris asks that teachers e-mail her or her assistants their plans. This has been a wonderful tool for communication and serves several purposes:

• It is simple for the teacher to send copies to all support teachers when e-mailing plans, thus distributing them quickly and easily.

• Teachers and their supervisors can keep electronic files, saving on paper and storage. This level of backup can be very helpful. On one occasion, an English teacher's computer hard drive crashed. She was devastated to think that she had lost all of her lessons. When the principal was able to forward all of her lessons to her from her e-mail files, hours of creative work were recovered.

FIGURE 7.1

Essential Features of Lesson Plans for Heterogeneous Classes

1. *A clear, well-articulated instructional objective.* The objective should include both the content to be learned and student behavior that will demonstrate learning. Reading lesson objectives can be a quick way to ascertain whether all teachers in the same grade level or all teachers teaching the same course are moving at a similar pace.
2. *A short summary of procedures that explains how the objective will be accomplished.* This can be as simple as a bulleted list or as elaborate as the detailing of a "do now" activity, a practice activity, and a closure activity. The level of detail required will depend upon the expertise and development of the teacher. For example, you may want to ask for more detail from a beginning teacher and less from a veteran. We suggest that even a short description, however, should include a description of how the teacher will differentiate instruction.
3. *Defined roles for in-class support personnel.* If there is a special education teacher, an enrichment teacher, an academic support teacher, or a teaching assistant in the room, that teacher's role should be defined in the lesson plan.

• The principal or assistant principal can easily comment, commend, or ask a question, thus opening a dialogue about the lesson and future lessons with the teacher.

• If teachers engage in team planning, copies of the lessons can be readily distributed among members of the team.

Observation in the Detracked Classroom

Well-designed lessons come to life in the classroom. Think of lesson study again. The process does not end with the design of the lesson. Only after the lesson is taught and observed by the team can it be critiqued and modified.

In all schools, observing and coaching teachers are important components of instructional leadership. In a school that is eliminating tracking, observations are perhaps even more important. They are the vehicle by which school leaders can evaluate whether instruction is changing to meet the needs of all learners. It is only in the classroom that the level of engagement of students can be evaluated. Do some students look bored? Are others falling behind or confused? Are English language learners included? Observations should focus on both the teacher and the learners.

Many schools use a combination of written formal observations—sometimes announced, other times not—and short, informal drop-by or walk-through observations of teaching. Both types provide critical information, and both can be used to shift traditional practices to constructivist practices that promote differentiation in heterogeneous classes. Below are the things we look for when we formally observe lessons taught to heterogeneous classes.

A clear, articulated learning objective. Certainly, the observer would expect the lesson to have a clear learning objective. And unless it is a discovery lesson, the observer would expect that the teacher communicate that objective to the class. We ask teachers to write the objective or the essential question of the lesson on the board. Posted objectives help students organize their thoughts and their notes, and their presence will certainly not hurt any learner. We know this from student feedback. When teachers have not written the objective on the board, some of our high school students have actually asked them to do so! They use it as a tool to organize their notes. When a teacher gives a list of topics for an exam, the students can cross-reference the list with the objectives in their notes to study for the exam. And because objectives are behavioral, students even know what the teacher is asking them to do to demonstrate their learning. Even as you, the reader, rely on the subheadings in this text to find the section that you want to read, lesson objectives in a student notebook can do the same for students. For a student who comes into the classroom a few minutes late, or for the student who has attention deficit disorder, the posted objective can help the student focus or refocus. Perhaps high achievers do not need to see the objective, but its presence on the board certainly does not hurt them.

The use of varied modalities for both teacher and student presentations. Lectures, with scattered board notes, do not work for all learners. If the teacher uses a direct instruction model to present information, the observer should expect some variation in the presentation of information. If students are asked to read (and we suggest that they should be reading silently), the teacher should inform them of the purpose for reading (using at least one of the strategies described in Chapter 5) and follow up with at least a discussion and note taking. If the teacher lectures, he or she should provide an organizer for students to take notes, a written summary of highlights, or a short film clip to illustrate the point. An assignment of reading homework can help students internalize what was told to them in class. Asking students to pair up and clarify their questions or to summarize what they have learned in a quick Think-Pair-Share forces students to process what they have heard. And of course, all instruction should be focused on achieving the lesson objective.

Differentiation of materials/practice by skill or achievement. It is unrealistic to expect each student to have his or her own individualized worksheet or reading materials. But some differentiation can be done quickly and easily. Not every problem needs to be completed by every student in a math or physics class. Different problems at differing levels of difficulty or complexity can be assigned to different groups of learners. As students explain their solutions to the class or to each other in heterogeneous groups, all students become familiar with each problem and its solution. We have also seen teachers differentiate reading materials on the same topic by reading level. This technique, while time-consuming, is highly effective in engaging all learners in the content. School librarians are excellent resources for finding such materials for teachers.

When students are solving problems, alone or in groups, cue cards with "hints" to lead students to the solution can be passed out as needed as teachers circulate around the room. Likewise, challenging problems can be given out to students who finish early. Observers should note whenever differentiation occurs and how effective it was in assisting students. The most important measure is the level of engagement of all students in the lesson.

Questioning techniques. Noting how skillfully a teacher checks for understanding is a part of any formal observation. It has long been established that wait time is essential to making sure that students have the opportunity to access memory and formulate thoughtful answers. By increasing wait time from five to seven seconds at the elementary level, and three to five seconds at the secondary level, the number, length, frequency, and creativity of student responses increases (Rowe, 1987). Wait time also increases the chances that lower-achieving students will respond to questions. Stahl (1990) expanded on the concept of "wait time" and renamed it "think time." He posits that it should include all periods of silence during the lesson that give students the time that they need to process information. Adding three seconds of "think time" during a lecture, for example, can give students time to construct new knowledge, formulate questions, and make connections with previously learned information. The benefits will vary by the learner. During wait time, asking students to jot down an answer or key word can help the teacher assess the understanding of a struggling student. She can then confidently call on the student to answer the question. For students who struggle and for those who are English language learners, think time gives the time they need for understanding. For high achievers, think time allows the acquisition of a deeper understanding and the formation of critical questions. The observer notes both the instances when think time is used and the effect of its use on different learners in the class, thus providing the teacher with vital feedback.

It is important that the kinds of questions used by the teacher be noted during an observation as well. When all questions are at the knowledge or understanding level of Bloom's taxonomy, critical thinking is neglected. Questions that ask students to analyze, synthesize, and form opinions grounded in factual information provide a rich texture to classroom discussion and capture the interest of students. While it is assumed that including activities that promote critical thinking will engage the higher achiever, research has shown that nearly all students are capable of critical thinking from very early ages (Willingham, 2007). This provides an added benefit in heterogeneous classes, where students of varied backgrounds have the opportunity to hear each other's perspectives. Finally, it is important that observers note who is answering questions and who is not. Counts by gender, ethnicity, and even location in the room can give the teacher valuable information about class participation. Observers can use a seating chart as an easy way to record information.

The following questions can help focus observations in heterogeneous classes and serve as questions for teacher self-reflection:

1. Is there a clear learning objective linked with the curriculum? Are all activities congruent with that objective? Can students articulate what they are learning?

2. Does the teacher foster the construction of knowledge by facilitating the transfer of former knowledge and life experiences to the new learning? Are there sufficient opportunities for students to process, question, record, practice, and show what they know? What is the balance between teacher talk/work and student talk/work?

3. Are all voices heard in discussion? Is wait time sufficient to promote active processing of information? Is there a good balance between questions that check for knowledge and questions that require critical thinking?

4. Is there differentiation in the lesson? Are some materials/activities tailored for the differing needs of students? Is new material presented

using differing modalities? Do students show what they have learned in different ways?

5. Do all adults in the room have a significant role in the lesson?

Short, Informal Visits to Classroom

Frequent and short walk-through and drop-by observations of teaching have become popular in recent years. Some approaches suggest 5- to 15-minute visits that focus on teaching strategies, while other approaches, most notably the Downey walk-through model, recommend 3-minute visits. The Downey model (Downey, Steffy, English, Frase, & Poston, 2004) focuses primarily on learning about the school and the implementation of curriculum, providing no evaluation of the teacher.

Whether you choose to stay for short visits or longer visits, drop-by observations can provide excellent information on the implementation of changing practices designed to meet the needs of all learners. Choose one or two important aspects of the reform that you would like to see become common practice, and then look for evidence of its practice in your visits. For a few weeks, choose active participation—are students engaged in an activity, or are they listening to teacher talk? Another focus might be evidence of differentiation. Another could be questioning techniques (wait time, level of questions, participation). The data garnered can then be shared with the faculty or with the leadership team. Such information provides a good indication of what staff development might still be needed.

Frequent walk-throughs also help school leaders get up to speed quickly on curriculum (Downey et al., 2004). It will be easier to see if a teacher is struggling with issues of rigor or clarity after visiting others who are teaching the same curriculum. You will become familiar with the rhythm of day-to-day learning and how students are doing. When parents who are concerned about detracking ask questions about curriculum or pedagogy at a PTA or Board of Education meeting, you will be able to address them with confidence because of your experiences in the classroom.

Downey suggests that reflective follow-up conversations should occur after most visits. Although not recommended by Downey, we have found that short notes or e-mails are also appreciated by teachers.

Communication Among Observers

When it comes to the feedback that teachers receive, consistency matters. There is nothing more frustrating for a new teacher than receiving contradictory messages from different observers. In some buildings, especially in elementary schools, observations are done only by the principal, and messages are therefore consistent. In other buildings, especially in secondary schools, principals, assistant principals, and department chairs observe. In some districts, central office administrators are also part of the process. In our high school, it is likely that nine different observers will observe a teacher during his or her first three years of teaching.

It is critical, therefore, that all observers communicate with each other and hold similar expectations. At the building level, the high school administrative staff meets once a week to plan observations and discuss what they have seen. Areas for growth are addressed, and areas of expertise are identified. All administrators are required to attend the summer teacher training when they come on board, and all are trained in differentiated instruction. Observations are guided by the questions listed in the previous section.

At each meeting, one administrator takes notes on the discussion. These are forwarded to central office personnel so that they are able to focus their observations on areas that the building administrators believe are important. Such logs are also helpful in determining areas in which staff development is needed. Just as communication among teachers is critical, so is it among school leaders.

Whether communication is in reference to individual teacher growth or implementation of curriculum, instructional leadership at both the building and the district level is key to a successful detracking reform. Schools that believe in access to excellence for all require vigilant leaders who are courageous in their defense of equity and innovative in instituting change.

Detracking cannot work well if it is implemented in a school culture where doors are shut and other adults rarely enter. Even as heterogeneous classrooms are communities of diverse learners, so the school must become a community of diverse adult learners. Schools where teachers observe each other, and where instructional leaders engage faculty in conversations about teaching and learning, are places where reform is more likely to flourish.

In such schools, faculties are open to trying new strategies and refining them—or even abandoning them—if they do not work. Teachers are accustomed to long-term supported initiatives rather than one-shot presentations by consultants. If you begin a detracking reform, you should make a commitment for the long haul. Every observation, be it formal or informal, should be an opportunity to discuss how classrooms can become more equitable places where all students have access to excellence.

8

....

The Essentials for Excellence with Equity

While reading this book, you have probably paused from time to time to reflect on your own beliefs about the purpose of schooling. Policymakers and philosophers have discussed and debated the purpose of public education since its beginnings. Economists and journalists opine regularly on the subject, and we cannot remember a time when there was consensus on this important question. Modern purposes include the following:

- To prepare a well-informed citizenry
- To prepare students for higher or continuing education
- To create a highly skilled future workforce
- To transmit appreciation and understanding of our cultural heritage
- To teach basic skills of literacy and computation
- To create a citizenry able to compete in a global economy
- To foster critical thinkers and lifelong learners

This list is certainly not an exhaustive one. When we ask parents what the purpose of school should be, the responses we get are usually far more individual and personal: "I want my child to be prepared for adult life." "I want my child to get into a good college." "I want my child to have opportunities that I did not have."

Not one of these statements of purpose is unimportant or without merit. And not one of the above—either the lofty purposes proposed by scholars and policymakers or the more practical purposes proposed by parents—requires that schools sort students into tracks. In fact, systems that sort and select, whether that sorting be called tracking, ability grouping, streaming, or leveling, make fulfilling those purposes more difficult to achieve. Although an education in high-track classes (in schools with adequate resources and good teaching) can fulfill all of the above, low-track classes with dry, basic curricula cannot.

So, what purpose does tracking serve in schooling? Tracking emerged at the beginning of the 20th century to fulfill a purpose that is not included in the above list—to sort students by perceived ability and to give them an education suited to their perceived needs (Kliebard, 1995; Lucas, 1999). Tracking was specifically created to respond to the influx of immigrants entering the United States in the 1920s (Hallinan, 2004). To cut to the chase, its purpose was to provide job training for new immigrants who were deemed "unready" for an academic education. Schools arrogated the right to decide who should pursue rigorous academics and who should not. When you think about the doors that open (and close) based on such decisions, the implications are enormous.

Beliefs That Sustain Detracking

The level of comfort that educators feel about tracking emanates from their beliefs about schooling, intelligence, and fairness, in addition to their personal experiences with the practice. If it is true, as we have argued in this book, that detracking is not merely a technical change but a school reform based on specific beliefs, what are the beliefs associated with detracking, and, more important, are those the beliefs that you hold? We have hinted at them throughout the book. It makes sense, as we close, to provide a summary.

Schools and Opportunity Matter

We are not so naïve as to believe that the socioeconomic and home environments in which children are raised do not affect their learning. Parental education, neighborhood safety, family income, access to health care, pre-school opportunities, and even parenting style are some of the factors that influence student achievement (Ferguson, 2005; Rothstein, 2004). Nor do we discount the significant effects of learning disabilities and natural differences in processing and retention, commonly referred to as "ability." We simply believe that the opportunities that a school provides, coupled with the efforts of the student, have an equally profound affect on student success. And most important, opportunity and effort are factors that educators can do something about.

We are troubled when schools respond to student needs in a way that exacerbates the societal or natural disadvantages that many children have. As Jeannie Oakes (2005) so aptly observes about lower-track classes, "It does not take a giant leap of logic to conclude that children who are exposed to less quantity and quality of curricular content and classroom instruction will not have their academic achievement enhanced" (p. 193). In short, when we consign students who have fewer resources to begin with to a lesser curriculum, they will surely fall farther behind. Schools thus intensify, rather than ameliorate, differences in achievement. When all students are given access to the best curriculum, and resources are put in place to support them, schools make a profound difference in learning. Think about what the schools of Finland have accomplished with their commitment to equity, described in Chapter 2.

Acceleration and Enrichment Improve Students' Achievement

The choice of acceleration, rather than remediation, is a basic tenet of a detracking reform. It is drawn from the work of Henry Levin's Accelerated Schools Project (1988), which demonstrated that enriched, accelerated learning experiences for children at risk of school failure produce gains in both reading and mathematics (Bloom, Rock, Ham, Melton, & O'Brien, 2001). This does not mean that teachers should never reteach a topic or reinforce prior learning in a support class. What it means is that skill-and-drill is not an appropriate curriculum for any student. If students are stuck mastering multiplication facts, teach them strategies, including the use of a calculator, and then continue to work on the basics along the way. No one should be placed in a skill-and-drill math class for the rest of his or her school career. Based on our experience, as well as the research of others, we believe that acceleration, rather than remediation, is the more effective strategy.

All Students Have Gifts and Talents

The STELLAR program that the district created was based on the work of Joseph Renzulli (1994), one of the preeminent scholars of gifted education. Likewise, Carol Ann Tomlinson, whose work in the field of differentiated instruction was discussed in Chapter 6, is a scholar in education for the gifted. Many researchers and educators have concluded that objectively defining who is gifted and who is not is a nearly impossible task. In addition, Renzulli and Tomlinson have found that the rich curriculum that they and other researchers have developed is good for all students. Within the context of such enrichment, a teacher seeks to build on each student's strengths, talents, and gifts. We believe that promise, which would have gone untapped if gifted education were given to only a few, emerges when all students are given the opportunity to develop their gifts and talents.

All Students Deserve Access to the Best Curriculum

In a detracked school, instruction—not curriculum and not standards—should be differentiated for learners in heterogeneously grouped classrooms. That is why we believe that a rigorous academic curriculum must be the default curriculum for every student. We are not alone in this belief. When governors from across the nation met at the 2005 National Education Summit on High Schools, their concluding report, titled "An Action Agenda for Improving America's High Schools," stated, "American high schools typically track some students into a rigorous college-preparatory program, others into vocational programs with less-rigorous curriculum and still others into a general track. Today, all students need to learn the rigorous content usually reserved for college-bound students, particularly in math and English" (Conklin & Curran, 2005, p. 11).

Although not every child may go on to take an IB or AP course in high school, each child should be prepared for this coursework. In fact, the National Research Council now recommends that schools develop "a coherent plan" to increase the numbers of students who are prepared to take IB and AP courses and that schools treat "all students as potential participants in grades 6–10" (National Research Council, 2002, p. 198). Our experience has demonstrated that this goal can be successfully accomplished by giving all students access to a rigorous curriculum.

The Achievement Gap Can Close

We firmly believe that achievement gaps result primarily from inequitable educational opportunities coupled with societal disadvantages such as poverty. We do not believe that bullying schools by fear and force will close the achievement gap. In our opinion, testing students repeatedly over time and then punishing schools for student failure is an ineffective strategy. And when elementary and middle school students are not promoted to the next grade, in an attempt to "scare them" into passing, ineffective becomes cruel. Neither do we subscribe to the close-the-gap "no excuses" philosophy that characterizes as heroes principals who threaten to fire teachers when their students do poorly on standardized tests (Heritage Foundation, 2000). It takes more than dedication and hard work for teachers and principals to raise student achievement.

However, we believe that the gap can close if we as a nation take equity seriously. We worry sometimes that the work of well-meaning educators and researchers who point to all of the societal factors that contribute to the gap inadvertently gives ammunition to those who want to thwart equity strategies. We cannot allow factors outside of the control of schools to paralyze us into inaction. As Ann Lewis (2004) points out, there are strategies that schools can use that make a difference. After delineating those societal factors identified by the Educational Testing Service (ETS) as adversely affecting learning, she states, "Almost half of the 14 correlates with the achievement gap that were singled out in the ETS report are under the control of school officials. It is up to them to establish a challenging curriculum, to make sure that poor students get their fair share of the most experienced and competent teachers, to ensure school safety, and to make sure poor students use technology in meaningful ways" (p. 101).

We believe that nations with gaps should focus on school policy and practice in much the same way as Finland did. They did not narrow their gap through testing and sanctions; rather, they narrowed it through equity policies, starting with detracking in grades K–9. But they did not stop with simply removing tracks. They adopted inclusive practices, created curriculum, and provided support for struggling learners (Linnakyla & Valijarvi, 2005).

As we have stressed throughout this book, detracking is as much a philosophy and approach to schooling as it is a technical change. Although detracking is a highly effective "gap closing" strategy for integrated schools, a philosophy of equity beyond detracking must be infused throughout our national system to help students schooled in underfunded, segregated schools that serve poor neighborhoods.

Schools Have an Obligation to Be Learning Organizations

Educators who are committed to improving schools are always frustrated when their colleagues resist reflecting on their own practices. The old adage that there are only two types of schools—improving schools and declining schools—is true. Schools need to engage in continual learning, and we believe that staff development and self-reflection are obligations, not "add-ons" to a school budget. If you seek to detrack your schools but do not believe in staff development and reflective practices, your reform will not get far.

Asking teachers who grew up attending tracked schools to differentiate instruction in heterogeneous classes is asking a lot. School leaders have the right to ask that of teachers only if they are willing to provide support. When one of the authors took on the responsibility of teaching her teachers a differentiated lesson in mathematics, she did so to send a powerful message: "I am in this too. I am willing to learn. And I am willing to put my commitment and expertise on the line in front of all of you."

If schools are to be true learning organizations, then all educators need to engage in the learning. When we institute a major staff development effort, our superintendent attends and learns alongside his assistants, principals, and teachers. Leaning must take place from top to bottom.

Teaching Requires Great Skill and Extraordinary Dedication

We are constantly amazed by the willingness of our teachers to go the extra mile for students. That attitude is not something that can be taught, and we are very lucky that such a culture of caring exists in the schools in which we work. We have learned from watching teachers who are skilled artists implement new strategies with ease. However, we have also observed that the teachers whom students love most are not necessarily those who are always the most skilled in our eyes. They are the teachers who personally invest in their students' learning and will go to great lengths to provide extra help for students whenever they can. When that dedication is combined with a deep belief that all students deserve access to the best curriculum and a willingness to reflect on practice, the teacher is a school treasure. We have yet to encounter a school that did not have such treasures among its faculty.

School Leadership Requires Vision and Courage

The fight for equity will rarely win you friends—at least among those who benefit (or believe that they benefit) from the status quo. Change is scary. "What if my child can't do the work?" "What if his SAT scores go down now that all students are in the honors class?" "Will I be able to teach this course the way that I used to, now that all students are in it?" "What if the scores go down? Will they still let me teach the AP course?" "I am a 22-year veteran and now I have to change my lesson plans?" These are but a few of the questions and fears that parents and teachers have when you embark on a detracking reform. Many are left unspoken, yet they smolder beneath the surface. Objections are raised that often have nothing to do with the worry (or resentment) that provoked them. Many people will give you excuses for why detracking will not work, but you might not hear the true reason for their opposition to the reform. Sometimes you will be personally attacked, and often your motives will be questioned.

The leaders of a detracking reform need to be courageous. They need a clear vision of an excellent and equitable school. When the opposition organizes, and it will, school leaders need to have the courage to listen, address as many concerns as possible, and then move forward if they are empowered to do so. By being well prepared with the strategies, research, and planning that we have presented in this book, the likelihood of success should greatly increase.

"Education Is the Fundamental Method of Social Progress and Reform"

These words are John Dewey's, and we believe them to be as true today as when they first appeared in his "Pedagogic Creed" (1897). When schools are determined to level the playing field for disadvantaged students and ensure that all have access to their finest curriculum, students begin to see college and career possibilities that before seemed out of reach. If you believe that the purpose of schools is to maintain the status quo, then detracking is not for you.

We are dismayed to see how racially isolated so many American schools have become. When classes in integrated schools are segregated due to tracking, the benefits of integration—and there are many—cannot be realized (Frankenberg & Orfield, 2007). If we are to progress as a healthy and socially just society, our children need to know and to learn from each other. The racial and socioeconomic stratification that tracking produces results in the loss of opportunity for such learning in many schools that are racially and/or socioeconomically diverse.

The following anecdote illustrates what we mean. Several years prior to detracking, one of our high school teachers was saddened by a remark made by a student in her IB English class. She was teaching Toni Morrison's *Beloved*, and a student raised his hand and asked, "Why do we need to read this? There are no black kids in this class." The teacher told the principal that while she was disturbed by the racially insensitive remark, she was equally disturbed that in an integrated high school, there were no students of color in her IB class.

A few years later, the principal was observing a detracked English 9 class. The class was analyzing a poem by Langston Hughes. As she listened to the insights provided by Byrant, an African American student in the class, she remembered the story told above. Every child in that class (as well as the observer) benefited from Byrant's thoughtful perspective drawn from personal experience. The diversity of the class benefited the learning of every student in it. Because of detracking, students of all ethnicities now participate in and contribute to the school's IB courses.

Success Can Be a Bountiful Harvest

Schools often operate on a scarcity model. In his research study of "star" public high schools, Paul Attewell (2001) argues that some schools limit access to honors and AP classes to enhance the chances of their most competitive students gaining entry to Ivy League colleges. He claims that schools use sorting and stratification to help some students "stand out from the rest" in the college admission process (p. 268).

According to Attewell, the reputation of the school is built on the few, and parents of children who are not top achievers are sadly disappointed with the education that their students receive. Furthermore, his study suggests that these schools limit access in an attempt to increase the average scores on high-track external exams so that they present an image of school excellence. Such schools operate on the premise that the resource of rich curriculum should be scarce and that the system should be structured to give advantage to its shining stars.

We have found that success can be bountiful. Although all students have access to our most challenging courses, our highest achievers still receive outstanding offers of admission to the most competitive colleges. Furthermore, we have learned that the experience of taking IB courses while in high school provides long-term benefits for students in college—and this success extends well beyond the "top" students (Burris et al., 2007).

A Review of the Three *P*s That Support Detracking

Detracking can begin in many ways. It might begin with moving away from self-contained special education classes and toward inclusive classes, or with giving all students access to an elementary gifted program. It might begin with the elimination of the lowest track or by opening the gates to an IB, AP, or honors program. No matter how it begins in your school, it is important to realize that true reform takes time, hard work, and commitment. We discussed the Three *P*s that inhibit reform in an earlier chapter; now we focus on the Three *P*s that we have found to be essential to a successful detracking reform: planning, patience, and persistence.

Planning

Planning begins when you envision what could be—and then the work of implementation begins. When our superintendent established the goal for the Regents diploma rate, he did not follow up by sitting back and seeing what would happen. He and his team began to map out needed systemic changes. He detracked the middle school. He eliminated the low track in the high school. He devised a system of examining the progress of each cohort of students as they worked toward a Regents diploma. He identified barriers to achievement and eliminated them. He supported professional learning so that teachers would be successful in heterogeneous classrooms. He put support systems in place so that students would be successful in heterogeneous classes.

Throughout this book, we have provided examples of the changes that were implemented in our district, from hiring practices to teacher observations. We learned along the way, and we abandoned strategies that did not work. Your plan may be different depending on the circumstances of your school or district. What is important is that you develop a plan and that the plan be guided by a belief system that puts excellent and equitable practices at the forefront.

Patience

Learning takes time. Both adults and children must have the space to process, ponder, and integrate new learning with old. When you propose a reform as all-encompassing as detracking, you are challenging a culture and practice that has been an integral part of schooling since the 1900s. You are disrupting the distribution of "high-status knowledge and learning opportunities," and that can cause great discomfort to those who believe that they benefit from the status quo (Oakes et al., 2000, p. xvi).

You are also going against the cultural "common sense" that says to sort students into groups based on some achievement criteria and then pace the curriculum accordingly. Only when you observe the effects of this practice does it become apparent that such a system does not best serve the needs of all students.

We are not arguing that your patience should be unlimited, or that you should delay the reform until everyone is on board. If you do, it will never happen. What we are saying is that you should not be surprised when you meet with resistance. We cannot tell you how many times initially resistant teachers and parents have "come around" after experiencing detracking and have acknowledged that heterogeneous grouping is so much better than the so-called homogeneous grouping that existed before. In time, as achievement rises, parents' anxiety subsides, and teachers see what a pleasure it is to teach detracked classes.

Persistence

Our superintendent, Bill Johnson, emphasizes the importance of persistence. It takes persistence to implement a successful detracking reform. Gently pushing through resistance is both a skill and an art. The key is pushing through without pushing people over. Always do your homework. You need to be ready to answer questions with honesty and with optimism. When parents or teachers raise valid concerns, you should address those concerns if possible, as long as doing so does not result in compromising the principles and beliefs of equitable change.

Our experience with persistence was that school leaders came on board first. Then teachers became believers. Then teachers became reform leaders. Parents were willing to give the reform a chance, and most, although not all, became believers. In a district in Maryland, parents demanded detracking, then teachers became partners in the reform, and finally the administration started to engage in change. No matter how detracking begins, if its advocates persist, change is likely to happen. Don't wait for strokes and accolades; advocate for detracking because you know it is educationally sound and socially just.

Concluding Remarks

In 1892, the National Education Association's Committee of Ten was appointed to grapple with the issues of what college entrance criteria should be and how public schools should best prepare students for college. Social changes, as well as the growth of American cities, had resulted in more students having access to high school. As the renowned educational historian Herbert Kliebard (1995) notes in his study of the growth of American curriculum, the committee was firm in its belief that all students "were entitled to the best ways of teaching the various subjects" and that "education for life" is "education for college" (p. 11).

According to Kliebard, the chairman of the committee, Charles W. Eliot, who was then president of Harvard University, was especially firm on this principle. He weathered the criticism of those who believed that there was a "great army of incapables" entering the public school system (p. 13). He fought against the notion that the school should sort and select adolescents and provide them with differing curriculum based on the school's perception of their future careers.

Unfortunately, in the 20th century the thinking of Eliot and the Committee of Ten was left by the wayside, and schools became the sorters and selectors of student destinies (Kliebard, 1995). The prediction of destinies, and the tailoring of curriculum to reinforce these predictions, became the model for schooling.

Eliot (1905) asked a simple question that is profound in its implications: "Who are we to make these prophecies?" (p. 331). This is the same question that we have asked you to grapple with throughout this book. Who are we to decide who gets access to the best curriculum the school has to offer? Who are we to decide that only the best students get the best teachers? How can we, as the leaders of socially just, democratic institutions, consign some students to lesser educational opportunities? And finally, how can we rest easy with a system that allows the racial and socio-economic stratification of its students?

Throughout this book, we have provided examples of how a school can detrack without sacrificing excellence. When you begin to detrack your school in small or great ways, you learn that excellence and equity are not mutually exclusive, and that both can thrive. And, after all, without equity, how can a school ever *truly* be excellent?

Appendix A

Growth Portfolio Model for Student Self-Reflection

Self-reflection is essential to learning. John Dewey once said, "We do not learn from experience, we learn from reflecting on experience." This portfolio for English 10A will help you reflect on your own learning as you archive specific assignments, revise writing, and examine your personal development as an individual learner. You will strive to meet the following specific objectives:

Objectives
☐ To become self-reflective learners
☐ To improve writing and test-taking skills
☐ To practice organizational skills
☐ To make choices and take control of your own learning
☐ To celebrate accomplishments and create personal academic goals

Procedure
You will archive major assessments for each marking quarter. After each assessment is returned in class, your teacher will provide an opportunity for you to review your work and write a quick reflection on the assignment, focusing on your strengths, weaknesses, and goals. Afterward, you will add the assessment and reflection to your portfolio. In addition, this portfolio provides an opportunity for you to submit creative writing and free writing.

At the end of each quarter, you will organize your portfolio according to specific guidelines, and your portfolio will be assessed accordingly. This will count as a major grade. You will meet with your teacher a minimum of two times per year for formal writing conferences.

Reflection Guidelines

Quick reflection. After each major exam and writing assignment, you will write a reflection on your experience based on the following topics:
☐ Strength(s)
☐ Weakness(es)
☐ Goal(s)

Source: Adapted with permission from a rubric retrieved August 16, 2007, from http://rockville.ny.schoolwebpages. com/education/components/scrapbook/default.php?sectiondetailid=4376&pagecat=357.

Reflective letter. At the end of each marking quarter, you will review the work you have completed and write a formal reflection letter using the following prompts (be sure to substantiate your assessments):

- ☐ My portfolio shows that my strengths as a writer are . . .
- ☐ My portfolio shows that my weaknesses as a writer are . . .
- ☐ My favorite piece of work is . . . because . . .
- ☐ I think I have grown as a writer because . . .
- ☐ Next marking quarter I plan to work on . . .

Content

1st–4th marking quarters

- ☐ Table of contents
- ☐ Mandated writing/quick reflections
- ☐ Mandated exams/quick reflections
- ☐ Revision: one formal revision of mandated writing
- ☐ Free choice: poem, "do now" activity, song, prose, essay, or other creative work

Appendix B

Rubric for Differentiation

	Evidence of a High Level of Differentiation	Evidence of a Moderate Level of Differentiation	Predominantly Uniform Instruction
Engagement and Participation	Students may approach the lesson from 3–5 possible entry points, which reflect the varying levels of achievement and multiple intelligences in the classroom. Nearly all students are actively engaged and on task throughout the lesson, and the teacher brings students back to the lesson when they are off task. The majority of the lesson is spent on students actively constructing learning. Student tasks and responsibilities vary. Student questions, responses and group activities are focused on the achievement of the lesson objective. Nearly all students are able to articulate what they are doing and why it is important.	Students may approach the lesson from at least 2 entry points, which reflect the varying levels of achievement or multiple intelligences in the classroom. Most students are actively engaged and on task during most of the lesson, and the teacher brings students back to the lesson when they are off task. There is an equal distribution of teacher talk/work and student talk/work. Student questions, responses, and group activities are usually focused on the achievement of the lesson objective. There is some variety in student tasks or responsibilities. The majority of students are able to articulate what they are doing and why it is important.	Students have only 1 entry point from which they may approach the lesson. The teacher tells students what to do, and individual student participation depends upon the student's level of motivation. The teacher makes minimal effort to bring off-task students back to the lesson. The lesson is dominated by teacher talk. There is a clear lesson objective, but only some students can articulate why it is important. Everyone is doing the same task.
Materials	Materials are open-ended, allowing for student choice and creativity, or are differentiated by achievement or intelligences. All materials contribute to mastery of the learning objective.	Some materials are open-ended, allowing for student choice and creativity, or are differentiated by achievement or intelligences. Materials are connected to the achievement of the learning objective.	Materials are uniform. They may or may not be aligned with the lesson objective, or they vary but are not connected to the achievement of the learning objective.

Questions	Questions and problems are tiered in a challenging manner, allowing all students to contribute to the discussion as learning is being constructed. Wait time is ample. Follow-up questions encourage clarification or expansion of learning. Students respond in a variety of ways—orally, in writing, sharing with peers, etc. Questions that challenge highly motivated learners are included.	Questions and problems are tiered but may not always be at the appropriate level or may be distributed ineffectively. There is sufficient wait time. There are some follow-up questions to encourage clarification or expansion of learning. Students respond in more than one way during the lesson—in writing, sharing with peers, etc.	Questions are similar in form, level, and style. Wait time may or may not be used. Follow-up questions do little to clarify or expand. Few students answer questions.
Assessments of Learning and Independent Practice	Rubrics are designed with the learning objective in mind so that students may clearly see what is expected of them to be successful on a given task. OR Students are provided the opportunity to choose from a variety of assessment methods that appeal to their own individual strengths and interests while remaining valid and appropriate for the material being covered.	A rubric is provided, although it may be too vague to clearly convey what is expected of the learner. OR Students have some choice of assessment methods, but those choices may be limited or inappropriate for the information or skills being learned.	No rubric is provided. OR There is no opportunity for student choice regarding form or method of assessment.

Source: Developed by Carol Corbett Burris, Christine Brown, and Keith Garrache, South Side High School, Rockville Centre, New York.

References

Andrews, L. (2007). Comparison of teacher educators' instructional methods with the constructivist ideal. *The Teacher Educator, 42*(3), 157–184.

Ascher, C. (1992). Successful detracking in middle and senior high schools. *ERIC Clearinghouse on Urban Education Digest, 82.* Retrieved May 27, 2007, from http://www.ericdigests.org/1992-1/senior.htm

Attewell, P. (2001). The winner-take-all high school: Organizational adaptations to educational stratification. *Sociology of Education, 74,* 267–295.

BBC News. (2004). Finland tops global school table. Retrieved July 9, 2007, from http://news.bbc.co.uk/2/hi/uk_news/education/4073753.stm

Bloom, B. (1956). *Taxonomy of educational objectives.* New York: David Mackey.

Bloom, H. S., Rock, J., Ham, S., Melton, L., & O'Brien, J. (2001). *Evaluating the accelerated schools approach: A look at early implementation and impacts on student achievement in eight elementary schools.* New York: Manpower Demonstration Research Corporation.

Boaler, J. (2006). How a detracked mathematics approach promoted respect, responsibility and high achievement. *Theory into Practice, 45*(1), 40–46.

Brewer, D. J., Rees, D. I., & Argys, L. M. (1995). Detracking America's schools: The reform without cost? *Phi Delta Kappan, 77,* 210–212, 214–215.

Burris, C. C. (2003). Providing accelerated mathematics to heterogeneously grouped middle-school students: The longitudinal effects on students of differing initial achievement levels. *Dissertations Abstracts International, 64*(5), 1570.

Burris, C. C., Heubert, J., & Levin, H. (2006). Accelerating mathematics achievement using heterogeneous grouping. *American Educational Research Journal, 43*(1), 103–134.

Burris, C. C., & Welner, K. G. (2005). Closing the achievement gap by detracking. *Phi Delta Kappan, 86*(8), 594–598.

Burris, C. C, Welner, K. G., Wiley, E., & Murphy, J. (2007). A world-class curriculum for all. *Educational Leadership, 64*(7), 53–56.

Burris, C. C., Wiley, E., Welner, K. G., & Murphy, J. (2008). Accountability, rigor and detracking: Achievement effects of embracing a challenging curriculum as a universal good for all students. *Teachers College Record, 110*(3), 571–608.

Cavanagh, S. (2005). Finnish students are at the top of the world class. *Education Week, 24*(27), 8.

ChemBond Listserv [Online message board]. (2006). Oneonta, NY: SUNY College at Oneonta. Available: http://external.oneonta.edu/mentor/listserv.html

Chokshi, S., & Fernandez, C. (2005). Reaping the systemic benefits of lesson study: Insights for the U.S. *Phi Delta Kappan, 86*(9), 674–680.

Cogan, L. S., Schmidt, W. H., & Wiley, D. E. (2001). Who takes what math and in which track? Using TIMSS to characterize U.S. students' eighth grade mathematics learning opportunities. *Educational Evaluation and Policy Analysis, 23,* 323–341.

Conklin, K. D., & Curran, B. A. (2005). *An action agenda for improving America's high schools.* Washington, DC: Achieve Inc. Available: http://www.nga.org/cda/files/0502actionagenda.pdf

Coughlan, S. (2004). *Education key to economic survival.* BBC News. Retrieved July 9, 2007, from http://news.bbc.co.uk/2/hi/uk_news/education/4031805.stm

Culham, R. (2003). *6+1 traits of writing.* New York: Scholastic.

Darling-Hammond, L., & Loewenberg-Ball, D. (1997). *Teaching for high standards: What policymakers need to know and be able to do.* Washington, DC: National Commission on Teaching and America's Future. Retrieved July 14, 2007, from http://govinfo.library.unt.edu/negp/Reports/highstds.htm

Darling-Hammond, L., & McLaughlin, M. (1995). Policies that support professional development in an era of reform. *Phi Delta Kappan, 76*(8), 597–604.

Dewey, J. (1897). My pedagogic creed. *School Journal, 54,* 77–80.

Downey, C. J., Steffy, B. E., English, F. W., Frase, L. E., & Poston, W. K. (2004). *The three-minute classroom walk-through.* Thousand Oaks, CA: Corwin Press.

DuFour, R., DuFour, R., Eaker, R., & Many, T. (2006). *Learning by doing: A handbook for professional learning communities at work.* Bloomington, IN: Solution Tree.

Eliot, C. W. (1905). The fundamental assumptions in the report of the Committee of Ten (1893). *Educational Review, 30,* 325–343.

Elmore, R. F. (2006). Three thousand missing hours. *Harvard Education Letter, 22*(6) 8, 7.

Ferguson, R. F. (2005, Fall). Toward skilled parenting & transformed schools inside a national movement for excellence with equity. Paper presented at the Fall 2005 Symposium on the Social Costs of an Inadequate Education. New York: Teachers College, Columbia University. Retrieved July 14, 2007, from http://devweb.tc.columbia.edu/manager/symposium/Files/71_Ferguson_paper.ed.pdf

Finley, M. K. (1984). Teachers and tracking in a comprehensive high school. *Sociology of Education, 57,* 233–243.

Finnish National Board of Education. (2004). *Background for Finnish PISA success.* Retrieved July 9, 2007, from http://www.edu.fi/english/page.asp?path=500,571,36263

Floden, R., & McDiarmid, G. (1994). *Learning to walk the reform talk: A framework for the professional development of teachers.* Michigan State University College of Education National Center for Research on Teacher Learning. Retrieved June 14, 2007, from http://ncrtl.msu.edu/http/walk.pdf

Fore, C., Riser S., & Boon, R. (2006). Implications of cooperative learning and educational reform for students with mild disabilities. *Reading Improvement, 43*(1), 3–12.

Frankenberg, E., & Orfield, G. (Eds.). (2007). *Lessons in integration: Realizing the promise of racial diversity in American schools.* Charlottesville: University of Virginia Press.

Frey, M. C., & Detterman, D. K. (2004). Scholastic assessment or g? The relationship between the Scholastic Assessment Test and general cognitive ability. *Psychological Science, 15*(6), 373–378.

Gandal, M., & McGiffert, L. (2003). The power of testing. *Educational Leadership, 60*(5), 39–42.

Gardner, H. (1991). *The unschooled mind: How children think and how schools should teach.* New York: Basic Books.

Gardner, H. (1993). *Multiple intelligences: The theory in practice.* New York: Basic Books.

Garrity, D. T. (2004). Detracking with vigilance. *School Administrator, 6*(7), 24.

Garrity, D. T., & Burris, C. C. (2007). Personalized learning in detracked classrooms. *School Administrator, 64*(8), 10–16.

George, P. (1992). *How to untrack your school.* Alexandria, VA: Association for Supervision and Curriculum Development.

Hallinan, M. T. (1992). The organization of students for instruction in the middle school. *Sociology of Education, 65*(2), 114–127.

Hallinan, M. T. (2004). The detracking movement. *Education Next, 4*(4), 72–78.

Heritage Foundation. (2000). *"No excuses" for poor children not to learn, research shows.* Washington, DC: Heritage Foundation. Retrieved July 20, 2007, from http://www.heritage.org/Press/NewsReleases/nr041800.cfm

Heubert, J. P., & Hauser, R. M. (Eds.). (1999). *High stakes: Testing for tracking, promotion, and graduation.* Washington, DC: National Academy Press.

International Baccalaureate Organization. (2006). *Middle years program IB guide.* Cardiff, Wales: International Baccalaureate Organization.

Kane, S., & Rule, A. (2004). Poetry connections can enhance content area learning. *Journal of Adolescent & Adult Literacy, 47*(8), 658–669.

Kerckhoff, A. C. (1986). Effects of ability grouping in British secondary schools. *American Sociological Review, 51*(6), 842–858.

Kifer, E., Wolfe, R. G., & Schmidt, W. H. (1993). Understanding patterns of student growth. In L. Burstein (Ed.), *The IEA study of mathematics III: Student growth and classroom processes* (pp. 101–127). Oxford, UK: Pergamon Press.

Kim, M. (2005). It's time to rethink teacher supervision and evaluation. *Phi Delta Kappan, 86*(10), 727–735.

Kliebard, H. M. (1995). The *struggle for the American curriculum: 1893–1958* (2nd ed.). New York: Routledge.

Levin, H. M. (1988). *Accelerated schools for at-risk students.* (Report No. 142). New Brunswick, NJ: Rutgers University.

Lewis, A. (2004). Redefining "inexcusable." *Phi Delta Kappan, 86*(2), 100–101.

Lewis, C., Perry, R., & Hurd, J. (2006). Lesson study comes of age in North America. *Phi Delta Kappan, 88*(4), 273–281.

Linchevski, L., & Bilha, K. (1998). Tell me with whom you're learning, and I'll tell you how much you've learned: Mixed-ability versus same-ability grouping in mathematics. *Journal for Research in Mathematics Education, 29*(5), 533–554.

Linnakyla, P., & Valijarvi, J. (2005). Secrets to literacy success: The Finnish story. *Education Canada, 45*(3), 34–37.

Loveless, T. (1999). *The tracking wars.* Washington, DC: Brookings Institute.

Lucas, S. R. (1999). *Tracking inequality: Stratification and mobility in American high schools.* New York: Teachers College Press.

Macrorie, K. (1988). *The I-search paper.* Portsmouth, NH: Heinemann.

Mosteller, F., Light, R. J., & Sachs, J. A. (1996). Sustained inquiry in education: Lessons from skill grouping and class size. *Harvard Educational Review, 66,* 797–843.

National Commission on Teaching and America's Future. (2007). *Cost of teacher turnover report.* Retrieved August 24, 2007, from http://www.nctaf.org/resources/demonstration_projects/turnover/TeacherTurnoverCostStudy.htm

National Council of Teachers of Mathematics (NCTAF). (2000). The equity principle. *Principles and standards for school mathematics.* Retrieved January 2, 2007, from http://standards.nctm.org/document/chapter2/equity.htm

National Research Council. (2002). *Learning and understanding: Improving advanced study of mathematics and science in U.S. high schools.* J. Gollub, M. Bertenthal, J. Labov, & P. Curtis (Eds.). Washington, DC: National Academy Press.

Nelson, J. (2007, April). AVIDly seeking success. *Educational Leadership, 64*(7), 72–74.

Oakes, J. (2005). *Keeping track: How schools structure inequality* (2nd ed.). New Haven, CT: Yale University Press.

Oakes, J., & Lipton, M. (1999). Access to knowledge: Challenging the techniques, norms, and politics of schooling. In K. Sirotnik & R. Soder (Eds.), *The beat of a different drummer: Essays on educational renewal in honor of John Goodlad.* New York: Peter Lang.

Oakes, J., & Lipton, M. (2003). *Teaching to change the world* (2nd ed.). New York: McGraw-Hill.

Oakes, J., Ormseth, T., Bell, R., & Camp, P. (1990). *Multiplying inequalities: The effects of race, social class, and tracking on opportunities to learn mathematics and science.* Washington, DC: National Science Foundation.

Oakes, J., Quartz, K. H., Ryan, S., & Lipton, M. (2000). *Becoming good American schools.* San Francisco, CA: Jossey-Bass.

Oakes, J., Wells, A. S., Jones, M., & Datnow, A. (1997). Tracking: The social construction of ability, cultural politics and resistance to reform. *Teachers College Record 98,* 482–510.

Renzulli, J. S. (1994). *Schools for talent development: A practical plan for total school improvement.* Mansfield Center, CT: Creative Learning Press.

Renzulli, J. S., & Reis, S. M. (1997). *The schoolwide enrichment model: A how-to guide for educational excellence* (2nd ed.). Mansfield Center, CT: Creative Learning Press.

Robb, L. (2000). *Redefining staff development.* Portsmouth, NH: Heinemann.

Robb, L. (2004). *Nonfiction writing from the inside out.* New York: Scholastic.

Robb, L. (2006). *Teaching reading: A complete guide for grades 4 and up.* New York: Scholastic.

Rothstein, R. (2004). A wider lens on the black-white achievement gap. *Phi Delta Kappan, 86*(2), 104–110.

Rowe, M. B. (1987). Wait time: Slowing down may be a way of speeding up. *American Educator, 11,* 38–43.

Sather, S., & Barton, R. (2006). Implementing professional learning teams. *Principal's Research Review, 1*(5), 1–4.

Schmidt, W. (1998). Are there surprises in the TIMSS twelfth grade results? *TIMSS United States.* (Report No. 8). East Lansing, MI: TIMSS U.S. National Research Center, Michigan State University.

Slavin, R. E. (1990). Achievement effects of ability grouping in secondary schools: A best-evidence synthesis. *Review of Educational Research, 60,* 471–499.

Slavin, R. E., & Braddock, J. H., III. (1993). Ability grouping: On the wrong track. *College Board Review, 168,* 11–17.

Stahl, R. J. (1990). *Using think time behaviors to promote students' information processing, learning and on-task participation: An instructional module.* Tempe: Arizona State University.

Stigler, J., & Hiebert, J. (1999). *The teaching gap—Best ideas from the world's teachers for improving education in the classroom.* New York: The Free Press.

Teddlie, C., Kirby, P. C., & Stringfield, S. (1989). Effective vs. ineffective schools: Observable differences in the classroom. *American Journal of Education, 97*(3), 221–236.

Tomlinson, C. A. (1999). *The differentiated classroom: Responding to the needs of all learners.* Alexandria, VA: Association for Supervision and Curriculum Development.

Tomlinson, C. A. (2001). *How to differentiate instruction in mixed-ability classrooms* (2nd ed.). Alexandria, VA: Association for Supervision and Curriculum Development.

Useem, E. L. (1992a). Getting on the fast track in mathematics: School organizational influences on math track assignment. *American Journal of Education, 100,* 325–353.

Useem, E. L. (1992b). Middle schools and math groups: Parents' involvement in children's placement. *Sociology of Education, 65,* 263–279.

Vanfossen, B. E., Jones, J. D., & Spade, J. Z. (1987). Curriculum tracking and status maintenance. *Sociology of Education, 60,* 104–122.

Vermette, P. J., Foote, C., Bird, C., Mesibov, D., Harris-Ewing, S., & Battaglia, C. (2001). Understanding constructivism(s): A primer for parents and school board members. *Education, 122*(1), 87–93.

Wallis, C. (2006, Nov. 19). How to end the math wars. *Time.* Retrieved February 19, 2007, from http://www.time.com/time/magazine/article/0,9171,1561144,00.html

Weinstein, R. S. (2002). *Reaching higher: The power of expectations in schooling.* Cambridge, MA: Harvard University Press.

Weiss, I., & Pasley, J. (2006). Scaling up instructional improvement through teacher professional development: Insights from the local systemic change initiative. *CPRE Policy Briefs.* Philadelphia: The University of Pennsylvania.

Wells, A. S., & Oakes, J. (1996). Potential pitfalls of systematic reform: Early lessons from research on detracking. *Sociology of Education, 69* (special edition), 135–143.

Wells, A. S., & Serena, I. (1996). The politics of culture: Understanding local political resistance to detracking in racially mixed schools. *Harvard Educational Review, 66*(1), 93–118.

Welner, K. G. (2001). *Legal rights, local wrongs: When community control collides with educational equity.* Albany: State University of New York Press.

Welner, K. G., & Oakes, J. (2000). *Navigating the politics of detracking.* Arlington Heights, IL: Skylight Publications.

Wheelock, A. (1992). *Crossing the tracks: How "untracking" can save America's schools.* New York: New Press.

White, P., Gamoran, A., Porter, A. C., & Smithson, J. (1996). Upgrading the high school math curriculum: Math course-taking patterns in seven high schools in California and New York. *Educational Evaluation and Policy Analysis, 18*(4), 285–307.

Wiggins, G., & McTighe, J. (2005). *Understanding by design* (exp. 2nd. ed.). Alexandria, VA: Association for Supervision and Curriculum Development.

Willingham, D. T. (2007). Critical thinking: Why is it so hard to teach? *American Educator, 31*(2), 8–19.

Worsley, D., Fox, E., Landzberg, J., & Papagiotas, A. (2003). *Changing systems to personalize learning: Teaching to each student.* Providence, RI: Brown University.

Yettick, H. (2006). East of the tracks: How two urban high school teachers boosted achievement by integrating classes. *Headfirst: Education on the Edge, 4*(3), 1–4.

Yonezawa, S., Wells, A. S., & Serena, I. (2002). Choosing tracks: "Freedom of choice" in detracking schools. *American Educational Research Journal, 39*(1), 37–67.

Index

About the Authors

Carol Corbett Burris has served as principal of South Side High School in Rockville Centre School District, New York, since 2000. Prior to becoming principal, she was an assistant principal at South Side, a teacher of Spanish at the middle and high school level, and a school board member for 10 years. Carol received her doctorate from Teachers College, Columbia University. Her dissertation on her district's detracking reform in accelerated mathematics received the 2003 National Association of Secondary School Principals' Middle Level Dissertation of the Year Award. Carol has taught graduate courses on school reform at Teachers College, and she regularly makes presentations on the positive effects of detracking to school districts and research organizations. Articles that she has authored or coauthored have appeared in *Educational Leadership, Phi Delta Kappan, Teachers College Record, American Educational Research Journal, Theory into Practice, The School Administrator,* and *EdWeek.* A chapter on closing the achievement gap, coauthored with Kevin Welner of the University of Colorado, appeared in *Lessons in Integration: Realizing the Promise of Racial Diversity in America's Schools,* a volume edited by the Harvard Civil Rights Project. Carol can be reached at burriscarol@gmail.com.

Delia T. Garrity has been a public school educator for 37 years, serving as a math teacher, teacher of the gifted, mathematics department chairperson, curriculum supervisor, assistant principal, and assistant superintendent. Since 1999, she has been the assistant superintendent for curriculum and instruction in Rockville Centre School District, New York, where she provided the leadership in opening academic doors to all students and designed a comprehensive professional learning model for teachers. During her tenure as assistant principal of South Side Middle School in Rockville Centre, Delia facilitated the school's transformation from a tracked system to one that offers all students an honors curriculum in heterogeneous classes. She received the New York State Middle School Assistant Principal of the Year Award in 1996. She has taught graduate courses on mathematics education at Long Island University and regularly gives presentations on detracking as a model of successful school reform to local and national audiences. Delia has authored or coauthored articles in *The School Administrator* and *Arithmetic Teacher*. She can be reached at dtgarrity@gmail.com.

Related ASCD Resources

At the time of publication, the following ASCD resources were available; for the most up-to-date information about ASCD resources, go to www.ascd.org. ASCD stock numbers are noted in parentheses.

Downloads
Diversity, Equity, and Opportunity: An ASCD Electronic Topic Pack (#105107E)

Online Products
Toward Equity in Achievement: An ASCD PD Online Course by Kathy Checkley (#PD05OC47)

Print Products
Closing the Achievement Gap: A Vision for Changing Beliefs and Practices, 2nd Edition by Belinda Williams (#102010)

The Differentiated School: Making Revolutionary Changes in Teaching and Learning by Carol Ann Tomlinson, Kay Brimijoin, and Lane Narvaez (#105005)

Educating Everybody's Children: Diverse Teaching Strategies for Diverse Learners, Revised and Expanded 2nd Edition edited by Robert W. Cole (#107003)

How to Differentiate Instruction in Mixed-Ability Classrooms, 2nd Edition by Carol Ann Tomlinson (#101043)

Results Now: How We Can Achieve Unprecedented Improvements in Teaching and Learning by Mike Schmoker (#106045)

Videos and DVDs
A Visit to a School Moving Toward Differentiation (one 30-minute DVD with a comprehensive Viewer's Guide) (#607133S)

Educating Everybody's Children (one 120-minute DVD with a Viewer's Guide) (#600228)

For additional resources, visit us on the World Wide Web (http://www.ascd.org), send an e-mail message to member@ascd.org, call the ASCD Service Center (1-800-933-ASCD or 703-578-9600, then press 2), send a fax to 703-575-5400, or write to Information Services, ASCD, 1703 N. Beauregard St., Alexandria, VA 22311-1714 USA.